THE THREE FATES

An Alternative History of the Band Emerson, Lake, and Palmer

Alan VandenBrink

Copyright

Table of Contents

Foreword and Introduction

The common band history of Keith Emerson, Greg Lake, and Carl Palmer as Emerson, Lake, and Palmer (ELP) is (as of 2023) thusly and briefly written – after exploding onto the international music scene in 1970 at the landmark Isle of Wight Festival, the band immediately engages in a manic tour-record-tour cycle. Instant, massive, and consistent worldwide fan acclaim, (mostly) critical derision, and a blizzard of popular album releases (Emerson, Lake, and Palmer, Pictures at an Exhibition, Tarkus, Trilogy, Brain Salad Surgery, Welcome Back My Friends to the Show that Never Ends) lasts through 1974 when the band goes on an extended, well-deserved break. There is some activity from Keith and Greg in the form of singles in this interim, but ELP the band lies low.

ELP returns in 1977 with the uniquely structured double album (three individual sides, one group side) Works, Volume 1, and – stubbornly defying fiscal and conventional wisdom as well as the musical and cultural trends of the time – go on tour with their own, hand-picked orchestra and burn through the record company's generous advance at an astounding rate. The band is forced to jettison the orchestra early on in the tour under the strain of financial challenges related to various unexpected and uncontrollable misfortunes. ELP subsequently break up in 1979 following the release of what seems to be a less than cohesive album of scattered outtakes and filler material in late 1977 – the unimaginatively and somewhat inaccurately titled Works, Volume 2 – and the infamous Love Beach album of 1978.

Throughout the 1980's, Keith, Greg, and Carl worked in various solo and band situations, and two of the three individuals collaborated in various settings. Some of these are more successful, serious, and long-term than others (Keith and Greg/Emerson, Lake and Powell, Keith and Carl/3, Greg and Carl/Asia), but the three never properly reform as ELP until the recording and release of the Black Moon album in 1992. While touring heavily and consistently in support of Black Moon through 1992 and 1993, ELP's future plans then are a bit of a mystery as the band basically vanishes following reports of Keith's health struggles. In 1994 ELP release In the Hot Seat, a perplexing album on many levels; there is no tour and the band appears to remain in limbo. Just as quickly as they disappear, the band reappears in 1996 and tours through 1998, both as a headliner and support act.

When 1997's tour rolled around, Greg and Carl make serious references and drop hopeful hints in interviews about an ELP return to concept album glory. However, ELP break up again (for the last time) in 1998 with Greg publicly announcing his resignation from the band and Keith and Carl acknowledging, confirming, and accepting his departure. With the exception of various archival releases, special editions, and the expected legacy repackagings, nothing is heard from ELP until 2010 when they accept an offer for a one-off, headlining show at the prestigious High Voltage Festival in London to mark 40 years of ELP. Prior to High Voltage, Keith and Greg undertake a brief US tour playing ELP (and related) material in a stripped-down manner heavy on audience participation. Following High Voltage, there are discussions for ELP to possibly continue touring, but they lead nowhere.

Sadly, Keith and Greg pass away in 2016; Carl remains active musically with The Carl Palmer ELP Legacy and Asia.

Many ELP fans see the break in 1974 and the subsequent orchestral project of 1977 as flies in the ointment that – despite the general appreciation for Works, Volume 1 – ruined incredible artistic and commercial momentum. Everything – literally everything – that followed in ELP's history never had that consistent magic of the first years. Why the break? Why the orchestra?

The fans maintained – ELP was unique and successful and recognized for what they brought to the table, *as ELP was initially conceived and presented.*

Of course, it's easy as a fan to cast stones and have this 'they should've listened to so-and-so' or 'what were they thinking' approach. Does any fan have any idea of the pressures and expectations (personally and professionally) of being in a high-profile, stadium-playing band? Coping with the demands from management and the record company? Let alone the artistic and creative deliverables, how many people were dependent on ELP the individuals to keep the greater ELP organization rolling to ensure they kept their jobs? This is a life that is beyond just paying the mortgage and keeping shoes on the kids' feet; I surely don't claim to know.

It is a tantalizing thought for any fan of a band that suffers a set-back, a change in direction, a change in genre or concept, 'going commercial' (whatever that could entail at the time), a change in personnel (everyone's favorite band has probably had a personnel change, and of course, the one who was given the boot was the one you appreciated the most, and the band's output suffered as a result), or at its most cruel, an untimely demise: what if. What if, ELP didn't go on break; what if there was no orchestra, what if Love Beach had been given a bit more of the real ELP treatment...what if...what if...many, many painful what ifs.

As an ELP fan, I too have had many of those tantalizing 'what if' thoughts and moments. When reading the many interviews of any of the three over (and between) the band's history where they speak of the ideas, hopes, and dreams for themselves and the band that – for whatever reason – never came to fruition, there is a wistful feeling of: I knew they could have done it, kept doing it, *and it would have been great*. Yes, it is wishful thinking, but not without tangible grounds as the true history of their early years clearly demonstrates.

That mindset was the motivation for this book. As a fan of ELP who was too young to have witnessed and participated in their earliest glory years (my first ELP-related concert was Emerson, Lake and Powell in 1986), I made it my mission to devour whatever scraps and clippings/clips of reviews, interviews, and videos I could to develop that 'I was there' mindset. I sought to understand the unique traits and characteristics of ELP as individuals within the dynamic of the band when it was riding high, with all the ups and downs and missed opportunities (in their words and in my eyes) that followed.

Since interviews are the primary way for a fan of any band to find out what makes the band and band members tick, I decided to use that approach for the book. Basic knowledge of your subject, some creative license (yet also based on fact or facts), and a controlled imagination is what is needed to keep it grounded within relative reality and not devolve into absurd counterfactuals. A big motivation for the style I approached was to maintain what seemed to be an inherent aura of genuine goodwill (minus the critics) that seemed to permeate ELP's early days. What would it have been like for ELP to have sustained those amazing early years over a 'mere' three decades?

I have tried to do so with this alternative history book, as I have only focused on the good and positive and have purposefully steered away from the negativity and attacks directed not just at the band, but even at the individual members and of course the progressive rock genre in general. It didn't help, in that regard, that Black Moon and In the Hot Seat were released in the 1990's when the internet started coming into its own. Sadly, the most offensive and petty attacks seemed to come from a few, but vociferous members of the bands' own fan base or the greater progressive rock community, not necessarily progressive rock music outsiders as one might expect.

My personal disclaimer – there are many, many ELP insiders, archivists, and fans who know much more about ELP the band, the history, the music, the equipment, the individual members, and their various inner circles and related machinations than I ever could hope to. There is no doubt it would be easy for them to shred the various (if not all) scenarios and such that I've postulated with relative ease based on the real history of the band and perhaps some direct, personal knowledge as well. Some will say that I'm looking at it all through rose-colored glasses (with a special tint available only from 1970-1974); based on the content of this book I would say that is intentional, and for that I do not apologize.

I hope this proffered alternate view of the band's history will, in its own way, continue to remind us and prompt many, many more discussions of the unified groundbreaking vision, concepts, virtuosity, influence, and contributions of Emerson, Lake, and Palmer the band, and the individuals.

Alan VandenBrink

Prologue

Emerson, Lake, and Palmer

Alternative Historical Events and Timeline Departures

1970-1994

Timeline Departure 1 – Lucky Man is not included on the debut album, but on Tarkus instead.

While recording the debut album, the band realizes they are one track short as the sessions come to an end. Greg proposes his song Lucky Man and showcases it to the others, but upon hearing it Keith does not agree to include it as he feels it does not match well with the musical concept of the band and the material they have recorded thus far. Instead, Keith suggests a studio recording of Rondo which he had done with The Nice and which ELP had been performing live. Management supports this as Rondo is well-known and heavily associated with Keith who has the highest recognition factor of the three; they believe it will give ELP's debut additional profile. Greg does not agree and he is insistent about ELP establishing their own studio and compositional identity, and not simply being The Nice, Part II. For the album's final track, the band ultimately agrees to complete a studio recording of Preacher's Blues, an original track, which ELP had been performing live on occasion as well.

Emerson, Lake, and Palmer

Track listing

Side 1

1. The Barbarian

(Bela Bartok; arranged by Emerson, Lake, Palmer)

2. Take a Pebble

(Lake)

3. Knife Edge

(Leos Janacek, Johann S. Bach; Emerson, Lake, Richard Fraser)

Side 2

1. The Three Fates

(Emerson)

a. Clotho

b. Lachesis

c. Atropos

2. Tank

(Emerson, Palmer)

3. Preacher's Blues

(Emerson, Lake, Palmer)

Keith. The recording sessions were extremely enjoyable, as this is the vision I had
for the next stage of my compositions when I felt I had reached the end of what I

could do with The Nice, and it is very gratifying to see it come to fruition. Greg contributed some wonderful material, both musically and lyrically. One of his songs wasn't used, a sort of a folksy song which didn't fit too well, perhaps he'll rework it a bit. Greg didn't want ELP to do a studio recording of Rondo, and I understand that, he laid out a convincing argument. While in the studio and working on Knife Edge, I had mentioned that The Nice had played part of Janacek's [editor – Leos Janacek, Czech composer] Sinfonietta [editor – orchestral piece from 1926] before I turned it into what was to become Knife Edge, but it was never as popular or ingrained as Rondo, so it wasn't a problem.

Greg. As the sessions were going full speed ahead, I was aware we were running a bit short on time, it crept up on the others. I mean, we were all working like mad. We were somewhat obsessed and thinking, this can't fail, the expectations were too high, especially from ourselves. When everyone finally realized that we indeed were short of material, I submitted a rather simple song of mine featuring the acoustic guitar. Keith didn't see how it would fit, and after some discussions that we wanted our debut to reflect ELP and none of our previous bands, we decided on Preacher's Blues which we've played live. It is a band number, but it's a bit simpler and lighter, to help offset the intensity of the rest of the album. It's something we might do with our future albums, to include a bit of levity, you know.

Carl. Did we have any material left over? Not really, this reflects what we have and what we've been playing. Greg did submit a sort of acoustic pop song, I thought it could have been worked into something but Keith couldn't be persuaded, at least right then. We thought it more desirable to create than grab something from the dustbin or argue, and we were looking to get the album out as soon as possible to maintain the momentum we had since our live debut. So, we agreed to do a proper arranging and recording of Preacher's Blues which is an original band composition we've been playing.

Keith. Carl pushed for us to work on Greg's song, I can't recall the title he had, but it just didn't match with the material we had. We already had a sort of reflective piece in Take a Pebble, which has a nice acoustic segment. I'm always willing to try any music brought forward by anyone, absolutely. Perhaps this song of Greg's will fit in better on our next studio album. I've learned that the feel of an album's cornerstone piece, if there is one, can be a large indicator of how the other tracks will go. I'm not sure what the cornerstone track is on this album, but I think there has to be an overriding consistency among the tracks.

Greg. I'm hoping to showcase some more guitar on subsequent albums, as it is my first instrument, you know. There is of course the Take a Pebble interlude and The Sage [editor – from ELP's live album Pictures at an Exhibition] which are being played live and are always well received, but there's not a complete guitar song on its own, as such. It is, of course, a challenge for the band should we play a guitar centric song. How does it work live with the bass, or can I do it solo?

Greg. It was merely a coincidence that the opening tracks of both King Crimson's and ELP's debut, 21st Century Schizoid Man and The Barbarian, start with the brutal, distorted bass. There is even a bit of similarity in the general riff, but it's just what the song called for, really. Someone did point out that with the tranquil Take a Pebble following The Barbarian and the likewise subdued I Talk to the Wind following 21st Century Schizoid Man; it does display a trend of sorts. I certainly can't argue with that, ELP does focus heavily on extreme shifts in dynamics, but it works for us.

Carl. When we considered doing a guide track for Greg's acoustic piece, and when he played it for Keith, I was going to play along. But, there was a problem with the bass drum microphone so the kit was not fully available. It was in pieces, to be honest. Did that make a difference as to how Keith perceived it? I'm not sure. It is a lovely tune, and I'm sure it will be on an ELP album not too far in the future, perhaps our next studio recording, and I believe it will be a band performance.

Keith. I'm not too worried that we don't have what appears to be an obvious single, but I imagine Knife Edge or Preacher's Blues would be the best candidate if we had to choose one. ELP didn't receive interest or support from the record company in any form because we were thought to be a singles' band, or that we had a cache of singles ready to release. It was our live performance reputation and abilities that caught people's attention and that's how Greg and I first interacted musically as well.

Greg. Playing in ELP does make one think about proposing or submitting original material. Both Keith and Carl perform at a very high level, so you need to be sure you're putting your best foot forward literally every time. I think we have a bit of an informal and friendly competition going on between the three of us in rehearsal and recording. You know, it's like, Keith, where's that tricky organ line you used to do, or, Carl that drum fill is missing from the break. There's nothing like crafting a piece of music where it eventually reaches a level you're satisfied with, you might not be able to describe it, but you'll know it when you hear it or when you see or hear the others' genuine reactions. ELP is substantially less improvisational than King Crimson and perhaps The Nice as well, so we haven't yet encountered a situation in the studio where sheer spontaneity has offered any surprises.

Carl. I really was the only one who came from bands known primarily for their singles, and successful ones at that. I don't think that really will be the case with Emerson, Lake, and Palmer, at least for right now. Based on how the first album turned out, it's obvious that's not the direction we're going, and the record company is fine with that due to our live concert reputation.

Tarkus

Track listing

Side 1

1. Tarkus

a. Eruption

(Emerson, Palmer)

b. Stones of Years

(Emerson, Lake)

c. Iconoclast

(Emerson)

d. Mass

(Emerson, Lake)

e. Manticore

(Emerson)

f. Battlefield

(Lake)

g. Aquatarkus

(Emerson)

Side 2

1. Bitches Crystal

(Emerson, Lake)

2. The Only Way (Hymn)

(Emerson, Lake)

3. Infinite Space (Conclusion)

(Emerson, Palmer)

4. A Time and A Place

(Emerson, Lake, Palmer)

5. Lucky Man

(Lake)

Keith. I'm completely thrilled with the Tarkus record as it is everything I hoped ELP would do and be, and with the support of Greg and Carl once everything got rolling, it was exhilarating. It was hard work, very hard work, but that's not to say it wasn't enjoyable. Greg was brilliant with the edits; Carl's input was invaluable on the arrangements and providing the germ of the idea for Eruption. I'm hoping we've created a timeless piece in that it lends itself not only to a rock interpretation but also classical in the orchestral sense and even jazz as well.

Greg. Keith's enthusiasm was infectious and while I was not initially smitten with it, hearing the Tarkus suite in its completed form is a vindication of sorts, I suppose. I do hope that as impressive as the Tarkus suite is based on its sheer size, Side Two of the album should not be overlooked at all. In a way, I believe it's a stronger Side Two than the debut as Preacher's Blues was a bit weak unfortunately, or perhaps it was just slightly mismatched, not as refined. There is a thread of similarity with the debut with The Only Way and Infinite Space; it's like Clotho and Atropos part two, right? But, we all agreed that it is sufficiently different. With this record, I believe one could say it's consistent and everybody truly gets a chance to shine within the band or song's context.

Carl. I am beyond confident that for both the fans and for our contemporaries, we have delivered a stunning piece of work, historical even, if I say so myself. This is the development of ELP that we hoped for; there was substantial collaboration and there is unison playing throughout the entire record. While there are so-called solo spots, there are no pure solo pieces, if you will. Not that the debut suffered as a result, but the impact of all three of us consistently on all tracks, the effect is quite palpable and significant.

Carl. I was very happy to be a bit more involved in composing and arrangements on Tarkus than I was with the debut, which I still really enjoy. Keith and I shared a

15

writing credit on Tank, but that was essentially my drum solo bookended by two of Keith's themes, very different and distinctive, but complimentary. With Eruption, I might not have contributed any chords or melody per se, but I worked closely with Keith on the breaks, accents, and all the time changes.

Keith. Greg and Carl have been exceedingly kind regarding my initial rejection of Greg's song Lucky Man from the debut. Especially since, well...what can I say, I've been proven massively wrong, especially hearing it now in a completed state and seeing its chart success in both Europe and North America. It has given Tarkus even more momentum, if that's possible, or rather it's given it momentum internationally to match how the record is performing in England. Greg was kind enough to prompt me to play a Moog solo on the outro as a way to provide a matching end to the record that provides an equivalent to the beginning of the record, this kind of ethereal sound that starts Eruption.

Greg. I know Keith meant no ill will with his initial rebuff of Lucky Man, at the time he honestly might not have seen it as an obvious or predictable ELP track. He wasn't the only one in our inner circle that felt that way, and I don't mean Carl. Which, in all honesty, is understandable considering the rest of the material we had, and of course there was the stress of needing to complete the record. In a way perhaps it was a good thing that Lucky Man wound up on Tarkus as we had a bit of a weak, but amusing track that was a take on the Little Richard song The Girl Can't Help It. I don't want to say too much about it, but it wasn't that good. It really just captured us having a lark in the studio; it wound up getting the boot, thankfully. But, anyway, once Lucky Man came into being, and seeing the unique contributions we each could and would make, Keith was very forthcoming in supporting it as I saw fit, my vision of the song. It truly is, I believe, a tune identifiable with no one except ELP.

Carl. As good as Take a Pebble was, I believe Greg has set quite a standard with his solo compositions and contributions to Tarkus. I know some critics and fans have stated that Side One seems to be Keith's side and Side Two seems to be Greg's side, so where is Carl's side? Well, you might say that if you only look at the song credits, right? But we all contribute to the arrangement, which is vital and can be very impactful as to how the songs finally turns out, but it's not the same as writing a melody or words. I'm quite content with receiving credit on the Eruption and Infinite Space segments, which, for those that recognize my playing, can clearly see what I provide within the architecture of the band.

Timeline Departure 2 – Tarkus is never recorded, ELP split up.

Following the successful eponymous debut, Keith and Greg lock horns when Keith presents Greg with the Eruption motif as a foundation for the next album and Greg doesn't see its merits. Despite Greg's protestations, management is able to convince him to at least go into the studio and work with Keith as studio time has already been booked. After agreeing to do so, just prior to the start of the sessions, the studio suffers from multiple burst water pipes which flood the studio and ruin critical pieces of equipment; the band's deposit is returned and the studio time is canceled. Keith and Greg cannot reconcile their differences.

Keith. I've come to the realization that following the rather quick and unfortunate collapse of ELP, that perhaps a band format is not what suits me best as an equal member and composer, maybe only as a director. There was some musical frustration on my behalf with The Nice of course, and I really, really believed that with the Emerson, Lake and Palmer record we were setting the ground work for a sort of long-term legacy. Everything and everyone seemed to be totally on board, we were developing a vision. It is true that many of the tracks all have a heavy individual focus, Greg with Lucky Man, Tank with Carl, myself with The Three Fates. We had just started, really, creating a foundation for a true collaborative, songwriting style. Each of us was starting to understand the nuances and strengths of each other's styles, compositions, and input on arrangements, you know. But, even though it was so early on in the band's life, we were heading the right direction...I felt we were.

Keith. I was very motivated to be working, and to keep working with, the caliber of musicians that Greg and Carl are. Unfortunately, Greg was adamant that he didn't wish to pursue the sort of angular, jazz-influenced compositions I was presenting him with, or the framework that I was offering him within which to work. Carl, who was greatly inspiring, loved it, thought it was great and we regularly exchanged ideas, whereas Greg couldn't stand it and dismissed it. It saddens me, greatly. But, I will always have fond memories of the dove album and I will miss Carl's sunny demeanor. The enthusiasm of everybody after the Isle of

Wight and during those first recording sessions, it was an incredible time. Carl and I have talked about working together again in some form, but nothing has been agreed upon or arranged yet.

Keith. Yes, yes of course I already have gotten many questions regarding working with The Nice again, and I've heard a lot from the fans. It seems that we really struck a chord with what we were doing, and we haven't been completely forgotten yet. I really love the guys, but I don't know even if I were to approach them how they would feel, how accepting they would be right now. Maybe sometime down the road. Besides, Lee [editor – Lee Jackson, bass player for The Nice] is doing great with Jackson Heights and I really enjoy their music. What's interesting is that Lee now also focuses on acoustic guitar and singing, just like Greg. But, now with Emerson, Lake, and Palmer coming to an end as well, I'm on a bit of a broken trail...two bands...I feel a bit like a refugee.

Greg. The Emerson, Lake and Palmer album only scratched the surface of what we could have done working together or, working closer together. Keith seemed to be attracted to showing off, and playing difficult sequences for the sake of, or proving the mastery, of executing complex parts...bursts of music...rather than focusing on great songs. Take a Pebble, Knife Edge. With his skills, I understand. But, I couldn't see myself just marking time with musical gymnastics, there has to be some soul or emotion, a blizzard of notes can be effective, but a constant blur of notes becomes pointless. Besides, the deposit fell through on the studio time, so nothing was really lost.

Greg. I am currently exploring my options...talking to people...writing. I've been reading a great deal about the Viet Nam war lately, I believe it may become a strong influence lyrically. If I do go back to a band setting, and definitely as a solo performer, I also would like to go back to primarily being known as a singer and a guitarist. I enjoy bass and it obviously allowed me to leave my mark with ELP and King Crimson, but the guitar is how it all started musically for me, not to mention that the most popular track on the ELP record was my song Lucky Man, a guitar driven tune. I have been in contact with Bob [editor – Robert Fripp, King Crimson leader, guitarist], having sung on the Poseidon record [editor – In the Wake of Poseidon, King Crimson's second album] with Crimson, well, as a hired hand anyway. There might be something there since Johnny Wetton [editor – bassist and vocalist for Mogul Thrash] didn't come through. Of course, that is provided that Ian [editor – Ian McDonald, King Crimson multi-instrumentalist] and Mike [editor – Mike Giles, King Crimson drummer] are still willing and approachable. I haven't heard it yet, but I hear their collaborative record [editor – McDonald and Giles] turned out quite nicely, which isn't surprising.

Greg. Some people have asked me how I feel about having been in two ground-breaking bands that have released acclaimed debuts, and then both came crashing to an end. Well, [pauses] that certainly was not my plan or some grand design, far from it actually. But art...music...can create personal and group dynamics that literally change day to day, or even hour to hour. One learns to compromise just as much one learns to cope with a drastic change in lifestyle and expectations. When given a glimpse or choice one also has to stand their ground and adhere to their principles, and recognize the opportunity. The reality is that there were great differences between the untimely demise of the original King Crimson line-up and then Emerson, Lake, and Palmer.

Carl. When Greg first balked at Keith's suggestions for the next record, I couldn't believe it, and not just because I gave Keith some compositional suggestions! [Laughs] The first album I felt was truly splendid and the reaction just as much. I mean, such potential, gone, so quickly, and so drastically. I'm disappointed, but not worried, really, I'm not. My phone hasn't stopped ringing, if you know what I mean.

Carl. I do hope that Keith will finish the 10/8 piece we had envisioned as the foundation for the next album. Greg's dismissal of it may have taken the wind out of his sails, but I believe he is committed to it; how it all turns out remains to be seen. Keith has no shortage of ideas; this was something that became quite clear after establishing the band. It would have been nice to have a second Emerson-Palmer writing credit in my catalog.

Carl. Yeah, it's all so strange...very strange and disappointing really. The three of us basically left well-established, I would say, even quite successful bands to take on the Emerson, Lake, and Palmer challenge, and I say that in a most positive way. But, to go back to where we were, where I was, I'm not sure right now. It would depend on the personalities of course, and then of course when dealing with speedy, spiky personalities, it could all end in tatters very quickly. I mean, Vincent is a wonderful organist and composer, I know he's working on some private matters, I think it would be doable provided all the stars are aligned.

Timeline Departure 2A – ELP records Tarkus despite Keith and Greg unable to reconcile their differences.

Despite Keith and Greg not seeing eye-to-eye on Keith's conceptual piece, ELP agree to go into the studio as the studio time has already been booked and paid for. Knowing that Greg is not impressed with the Tarkus suite, Keith asks him for minimal vocal and lyrical input. Greg eventually provides lyrics and vocals on two Tarkus segments - Winds of Time and Stones of Years. Keith finishes the off the side-long piece primarily as an instrumental piece with the highlight being an extended, Moog-centered extemporization on the Aquatarkus segment.

Tarkus

Track listing

Side 1

1. Tarkus

a. Eruption

(Emerson, Palmer)

b. Winds of Time

(Emerson, Lake)

c. Iconoclast

(Emerson)

d. Manticore

(Emerson)

e. Stones of Years

(Emerson, Lake)

f. Aquatarkus

(Emerson)

g. Eruption - Reprise

(Emerson, Palmer)

Side 2

1. Bitches Crystal

(Emerson, Lake)

2. The Only Way (Hymn)

(Emerson, Lake)

3. Infinite Space (Conclusion)

(Emerson, Palmer)

4. Battlefield

(Lake)

5. A Time and A Place

(Emerson, Lake, Palmer)

6. Black Mass

(Lake)

Keith. The Tarkus record is now completed, it truly is finished. [Pauses] I am happy with it, very happy. On reflection, I see a great similarity between the Tarkus suite and The Three Fates [editor – from ELP's debut album]. I think Atropos [editor - third section from The Three Fates from ELP's debut album] definitely was a hint of what was to come with Tarkus, but not quite as rhythmically scattered. Although, I do think that at the time Atropos would not have worked in a full band setting, it was a pure piano show-piece. Thus, the big difference being of course I've brought in Hammond, Moog, and that there were actually what one could call proper songs, or song sequences, I suppose. I do think Greg's songs are very good on their own, but, it would have been nicer, you know, it could have been.

Greg. You really can see what ELP is capable of when you look at the songs, right? Just the songs. On the first record you have Knife Edge, Take a Pebble, on Tarkus you have Bitches Crystal, A Time and A Place. These are songs that you would only hear from ELP. I supported Keith and provided lyrics to two segments of his Tarkus suite because he had worked very, very hard on it, but then piecing together my songs just to make them fit in an abstract way...it wouldn't be coherent, it would be a concept in name only.

Carl. Strangely enough, Keith and Greg agreed to disagree, and while they may not have fully collaborated to the maximum degree on Keith's suite, it was successfully recorded. Greg gave Keith space and helped him out slightly on Keith's extended piece providing some lyrics and vocals, and Keith in turn supported Greg on his songs, and of course they composed several quality pieces together for Side Two.

Keith. I really thought we could have easily worked a couple of Greg's tunes from Side Two into the Tarkus suite and it would have been substantially more satisfying and complete and more reflective of ELP as a collaborative entity, that's my view. But, that's not how it went.

Greg. I respect Keith as a composer, he has tremendous skill and vision, but I didn't want to just throw things together. Battlefield and Black Mass are strong enough pieces to stand on their own, just as strong as Bitches Crystal. I fear these pieces would get lost or at least would appear to be lyrically ambivalent within the greater piece. Musically making them fit, with Keith's compositional abilities, we didn't see that as an obstruction. At the end of it all, Keith got to record Tarkus as he wished and I helped him, as I provided some more song oriented elements. If

24

you think about it, the germination of that thought summarizes the ELP debut record as well.

Carl. You reach a certain point as a band when you're working on a piece and there's this unspoken feeling or sense when everyone has done what they can do and it's time to move on, you just have to move on. You do this out of respect for the others and for the band, really. Insisting on endlessly thrashing out the same issues or asking people to do the same thing ten different ways just creates unnecessary tension and then the cooperation just vanishes completely. That is how it felt, to me, how it went with Tarkus. Working on the other songs was easy; we had great enthusiasm and cooperation, a constant exchanging of ideas and experimentation. Myself, I can hear it clearly in the Side Two tracks.

Keith. In this business, time is the most valuable commodity, time equals money, and time equals the ability to do what you want, right? Time, time, and more time. If we would have had more time, could Greg and I have smoothed out our differences? I believe so, as the two sections he contributed lyrics and vocals on turned out quite good, really great actually. But, we started out somewhat at odds even before we went in the studio, which made collaboration difficult, but not impossible as Side Two shows. When everything is clicking, the collaboration between all three of us is absolutely wonderful.

Greg. If you look closely at the first album and then Tarkus, you see a break from what made up the successful debut. For the first album we had a few collaborative works and then our more individual tracks. Let's say we would have mixed up Take a Pebble and Lucky Man with The Three Fates to create an extended piece. Is it possible to do that, yes, but why do so if there's no overall, well-grounded plan? One is just flailing about and patching pieces together. This is exactly why the first album was strong. Is it the future of ELP to have our albums consist of 50% individually focused tracks and 50% band tracks? If we're going to perform a conceptual piece, then we should create a conceptual piece and not just patch one together.

Carl. Despite Keith's and Greg's differences on Tarkus, I believe it will stand the test of time. It is ELP really pushing the boundaries not just of our own capabilities, but of our genre, call it whatever you'd like. The Eruption sequences are, in my opinion, absolutely fantastic and provide perfect bookends for the piece.

Keith. Carl commented that we unintentionally flipped the blueprint from the first album to make Tarkus, I wasn't sure what he meant at first, but I suppose I see it now. With most of Tarkus being my material on Side One and more songs on Side Two, it was the reverse from the debut where Side Two was occupied by The Three Fates and Tank, with Lucky Man being the offset and Side One was more song-oriented, you know. I try not to overanalyze, it worked out well for what we wanted to do on both records.

Greg. Side Two of Tarkus is a great example of what ELP can do within the framework of conventional rock songs using European influences. Bitches Crystal and A Time and A Place are as intense as any hard rock currently available, but then we have Battlefield to provide an oasis of calm and introspection, again, much like the well-received first album with Knife Edge and then Lucky Man providing the same counterbalance. Over the course of two sides of an album, you need equilibrium of material and a consistent, realistic representation of the band.

Carl. Not taking anything away from the Tarkus suite, but the material on Side Two proves that ELP can be concise within the framework of progressive rock. Yes, we will continue to focus on and expanding upon extended pieces of music utilizing European influences, but with the proper compositions this time we've proven we can perform and record using both approaches to all our compositions to great effect.

Timeline Departure 2B – Despite Keith and Greg not seeing eye-to-eye on Keith's conceptual piece, ELP agree to go into the studio as the time has already been booked and paid for. Greg brings in material and begins to formulate his own concept piece parallel to Keith's; Keith forges ahead on his composition. Initially, both agree to only play on each other's pieces and provide no compositional input; half-way through the recording sessions, both relent and help each other on one of the other's pieces.

Tribus

Track listing

Side 1

1. Tarkus

a. Eruption

(Emerson, Palmer)

b. Stones of Years

(Emerson, Lake)

c. Iconoclast

(Emerson)

d. Manticore

(Emerson)

e. Aquatarkus

(Emerson)

f. Eruption - Reprise

(Emerson, Palmer)

2. Bitches Crystal

(Emerson, Lake)

Side 2

1. Leaves of Sorrow

a. Black Mass

(Lake)

b. The Battlefield, Part I - The Season's Call

(Lake)

c. Oh, My Father

(Lake)

d. The Only Way

(Emerson, Lake)

e. The Battlefield, Part II - The Spectral Torch

(Lake)

2. A Time and a Place

(Emerson, Lake, Palmer)

Keith. If somebody would have told me before going into the studio that the approach we took with the Tribus record was going to work, I would have had some immediate questions. But, for all the unexplained reasons how things sometimes work out, this worked out. Greg and I had set some boundaries, which for co-writers might have seemed a bit strange, but it actually reduced the

28

friction.

Greg. Keith and I had no intent to shut the other out, we just agreed on basic boundaries based on what we both were bringing into the studio for the next record. If either of us would have sensed that the quality of the music was lacking, neither of us would have been shy. But, especially as the recording moved along, we both saw what the other was doing and how clever it really turned out to be. And of course, beyond the two extended suites, we teamed up quite well on two songs that are as strong as anything we've done

Carl. People don't believe me when I say that this album had great cooperation between all three of us. I was a bit more involved with Keith's side due to my contribution on the Eruption sequences, but neither Keith nor Greg never were sequestered. It was merely an agreement that they would provide leadership on their respective pieces. Just as easily, when it came to Bitches Crystal and A Time and a Place, it was simple to switch gears and work cooperatively.

Keith. We've certainly had our fair amount of criticism leveled at us about the album [editor – Tribus], maybe even more so than the debut. I imagine that it had to do with the hyper individuality that seemed to be even more pronounced. Even in retrospect, it really wasn't by design at all. We agreed to work separately together, if that makes sense, once we were at this impasse from the beginning before we even went into the studio. We didn't want to close up shop, you know, we knew we could still make it work.

Greg. In a way, Keith provided great motivation with his Tarkus concept. It might not have completely resonated with me, but I could see what Keith was trying to do, and when I looked at my compositions and recognized an unconscious theme or themes, it all made sense. Just as Keith could consciously string together themes or motifs, I could as well, but it's a different challenge with the added dimension of the lyrical considerations. I wouldn't necessarily say it's more difficult, but it is its own work.

Carl. This record certainly felt different at first, but then as we started fine-tuning the arrangements and then recording with Greg taking the lead on his piece and Keith on his, we all just said, "Let's get on, and get this done." I think both Keith and Greg had more than one occasional light bulb moment where they saw something in the other's work and recognized how good it was. But, rather than dredging up old arguments, the discussions became complimentary. I think the feeling was, more than anything else, that this band has a lot left in the tank.

Keith. I understand Greg's hesitation to merely glue some musical pieces together and let the words fall where they may. I mean, the lyrics are Greg's responsibility and he treats it very seriously. It is his commitment and obligation, and he does it very well. If the tables were turned and Greg was just telling me to cobble some music together, I wouldn't feel right about that, it was a bit of a revelation. It helped me temper my demands, and when the cooperation happened naturally, it was what I hoped it would be.

Greg. Recognizing the connection between organized religion and state power is nothing new. You can have something as direct as a theocracy, or indirectly in the form of money and influence, perhaps even corruption. I'm not saying that one is complimentary to the other every time or that it always happens, but there is a history there, especially in Europe, you know. The story I tried to tell was that you have the leveraging of emotion through religion to accomplish the state's goals or establishing control; this is what Black Mass is all about. Then you have the rallying and the propagandizing to go off to war, to fight this chimera, or to secure the state or its goals, right? In England I believe it was referred to as the balance of power. That is the two-part story of The Battlefield, the moral corruption. Then you have the real, human loss from placing this blind trust in statecraft, the propaganda, with Oh, My Father and the sad realization, what was this all for? And finally, there is The Only Way where one realizes they have to find their own path. I'm not saying which way to turn at the fork in the road, but at the end of the day, you do have to choose yourself, this is life.

Carl. Working on the two extended pieces was the biggest lesson I could have asked for as far as musically understanding Keith and Greg. Obviously Keith's piece is technically more challenging with the unexpected turns and unconventional changes, but Greg's piece required a lot of work as well. Just as much, really, but it required a different kind of attention. Rather than finding musical transitions which, in the case of Tarkus, could be very abrupt or even harsh, with Greg's piece it required more subtlety so it wouldn't be so jarring. In some ways, it was more of a challenge.

Keith. Well, we didn't want to have a row about the album title, so we agreed that it wouldn't be either Tarkus or Leaves of Sorrow, or from one of the individual pieces. We wanted to portray an agreeable front, evenhandedness. All of us took basic Latin in school, so why not Tribus? It is a pure coincidence that it is rather close to Tarkus, there was no issue there.

Greg. Both Keith and I agreed that the title wouldn't come from anything from either of our extended pieces; we didn't think one or the other should have greater recognition or dominance and we didn't have a single to reflect the tone of the album. I believe it was Carl's suggestion, and it turned out to be a great reference to the band itself.

Carl. I was looking for a title completely independent of the music, but that was a reflection of us as independent factors working together, a sort of balancing out. Calling it Three might have caused confusion as it was our second album, and we also wanted a bit of a futuristic feel based on Keith's music, but also something historical based on Greg's work. So, I thought why not use something that is mysterious and descriptive, but also has the look and sound of the past as well as the present.

Timeline Departure 3 – Tarkus' release is delayed.

Shortly after announcing that ELP would be releasing their second studio album Tarkus, there is a surprise announcement from the record company that the release has been postponed with no new release date provided. Management is quick to assure the media and the public that the band is not breaking up and that the record is ready to be released, but that the band wants the timing to be right.

Keith. We have such incredible momentum with this band, there's this buzz of activity, but...we have to be careful, you know. If we don't pace ourselves, in three years we'll be exhausted beyond comprehension. Management was quite up in arms at first, but we are lucky that the first ELP album was a smash and that Pictures [editor – ELP live album Pictures at an Exhibition] is mostly ready to go. It's tempting, very tempting, to immediately put out another album, for which we have much material recorded, written, and conceptualized. But, we want to make sure we can devote the necessary care and oversight that all tracks have the level of quality ELP fans have quickly become accustomed to.

Keith. When you are part of a band that is riding some success and the internal enthusiasm, I'm learning as a composer to restrain and channel what seems to be constant motivation and creativity based on what's happening right now into a form of anticipation. I want to place an emphasis on developing what is the originality and excitement that comes with inspiration into a well thought out and well-paced piece of music.

Greg. We are fortunate to have had what appears to be such instant success. What's not seen is, of course, the foundation of that success and artistic access was built up over many years of being a grafter; not exactly easy living, you know? For that reason we want to be very confident as we move forward that the band has a good understanding of where we are, where we want to go, and how to best get there...this is a marathon, not a sprint.

Greg. The current artistic climate seems to be very much aligned with us now in that a wide variety of music is given a chance. For us, at least we seem to have the appeal from a certain segment. Popular trends and such, I think while we're certainly not mass market, we have an element that identifies with our type of music. In a way, initial success gives us a bit of a breather, some space as long as we have a quality product to offer and of course the support of the record company.

Carl. Is there such a thing as too much momentum? We caught ourselves moving almost too quickly, right? We had a tremendous live debut, an outstanding first release, but we don't want to overextend ourselves especially since there's no real need to. ELP is far from being in survival or desperation mode. In a way, having constant anticipation within the band and amongst the fans so quickly within the band's initial formation is good fortune; there's no need to press the matter, those conditions will happen naturally.

Keith. Although we were sort of basking in the afterglow, you know, we took a step back and said, 'Two albums in the span of six months?' We need to pace ourselves personally and professionally, and as a recording artist one never wants to leave the pantry completely bare.

Greg. While ELP might be a new band, we as individuals are not at all new to playing at a professional level. Our management and the record company see this as well. ELP, in a relatively short time, already has a track record of good quality and consistency so when we make a demand for good reason, it's understood that there is a solid justification.

Carl. What's that American band, they played at Woodstock, I believe. Creedence Clearwater Revival? I was reading that they put out three albums in one year? No live albums, no greatest hits, three albums of new, original material. That is astounding considering the quality of the songs and their popularity. Admittedly it is different music than ELP, but still, I don't know. To sustain that kind of output you need not only significant artistic reserves but personal as well, that is quite impressive.

Timeline Departure 4 – Still...You Turn Me On from Brain Salad Surgery is released as a single in the US, and winds up climbing the charts as high as US #27, out-charting From the Beginning and propelling Brain Salad Surgery to US #5.

Keith. Is it ELP [pauses]? Yes, I imagine it is despite it being Greg's song and obviously his style, that is, his performance at the forefront with Carl and I supporting, somewhat. But that's not to say it wasn't enhanced once it was brought to the band. I don't know. I don't want to upset Greg or Carl who thought it wasn't quite as representative of ELP as a band despite Greg's signature voice which, as we all know, is and will always be the voice of ELP. But, I've come to accept that as long as the band is willing to tackle my lengthier compositions, why wouldn't I be for Greg releasing what might be interpreted as a solo song but is truly presented and promoted as ELP? And besides, it's a wonderful song, isn't it?

Greg. It's never my intent to create some kind of division within the band with my solo-oriented acoustic pieces. But, in all seriousness, Carl has more insight than the typical drummer in a band; he's not just a drummer as his drumming style and general understanding of musical structure leads to vast amounts of input on arrangements. I think what we have with Still You Turn Me On, what we have is one of my ballads in the format of Lucky Man and From the Beginning, which were both quite successful for the band. American radio pre-releases showed audiences were quite enthusiastic over it, so why not, why not release it? Sure, it is my song, but anything that elevates the profile of the band is not to the band's benefit, but to Keith's and Carl's benefit as well, and they both provided great input.

Carl. Keith was rather ambivalent about releasing Still You Turn Me On as a band single and Greg knew he would reap the long and short-term benefits; I mean, the band would too, of course. Greg was very open about his support in releasing the song, obviously. Of course I knew it would be a benefit to the band's catalog and chronicle. I mean, Lucky Man is great, and it was a band performance. From the Beginning, another great tune from Greg had even less drums than Lucky Man but was still a band performance, and now Still You Turn Me On, no drums; right. It's possible there could be more ELP songs without drums. Of course, Greg could say the same thing about songs not having guitar of which we have plenty, which is obvious. With Greg's focus on acoustic based material, it certainly is a possibility, we would have to see. I mean, he delivers some gems, so there's that. When you look at our albums and our live performances, I'm grateful for the potential and talent in this band, all three of us get a chance to shine on every record and at every show, it's a rarity for a band. I may have to start writing more percussion centric pieces or something someday.

Timeline Departure 5 – Jerusalem, the lead-off track from ELP's Brain Salad Surgery album, is released as a single in the UK and becomes ELP's highest charting single to date at #9 and propels Brain Salad Surgery to UK #1, ELP's second UK #1 album following Tarkus.

The BBC, which had initially banned ELP's version of leadoff single Jerusalem upon the release of the Brain Salad Surgery album in November of 1973, reconsiders their decision after meeting with the band and its management. Satisfied with ELP's claims that it was their sincere intent with Jerusalem to record and present it with respect and reverence for British tradition and history and treating it like the national iconic hymn it is, the BBC rescinds their ban. By Christmas time, Jerusalem is a UK top-10 hit for ELP.

Keith. It is a great relief that the BBC agreed to review our petition to rescind the ban on Jerusalem; this was no rock and roll mischief, none at all. We are British and any version of Jerusalem will stir the heart of any true Brit like it does ours. I would understand if they saw the album cover to Brain Salad Surgery and someone very conservative...well, they're all quite conservative at the BBC...would say well, oh dear, this is a bit much, I'm sorry. I would even completely understand if they looked back at my youthful indiscretions with The Nice at the Royal Albert Hall and say, what? Him? This guy again? Didn't we put him in the cupboard? Who let him out? But, Jerusalem was done by ELP with the absolutely highest regard, and I believe it shows.

Greg. Jerusalem is one of those rare songs, or hymns if you will, that has something for everyone. Grand music, a moving melody, stirring lyrics, one probably doesn't need to be religious or even British to be taken in by it, but I imagine it probably helps. Of course, we are fortunate that it translates so well to Keith's abilities on the Hammond, and the wonderful trumpet sounds on the Moog. When I heard Keith's first passes on the Moog I instantly thought of Clarke's [editor – Jeremiah Clarke, English baroque composer] Trumpet Voluntary. Some fans have told us that it also has elements that remind them of Penny Lane [editor – Beatles song]. So there you go, British influences and reflections everywhere, from top to bottom.

Carl.   What else can you say, as Jerusalem has been and continues to be a magnificent piece of music and part of the British tradition. We spent many, many hours getting Jerusalem right, not just with recording it, but with the mixing as well. We all agreed it had to be done with absolute honesty and integrity; we wouldn't have accepted anything less. We don't necessarily feel vindicated that it hit the charts, which is nice of course, but more so that people can sense that we treated the tune with genuine regard. And of course, we'll continue to do so live as well.

Timeline Departure 6 – ELP do not release Works, Volume 1, due to unresolved differences between Keith and Greg. The band goes on hiatus pending Keith and Greg resolving their individual concerns. Unexpectedly, Carl releases a solo album.

Just prior to embarking on the recording sessions for Pirates, Keith and Greg come to an impasse regarding the upcoming tour plans, even before the recording sessions are complete for the album that eventually came to be known as Works, Volume 1. Contentious feelings regarding the orchestral issue, which had been simmering in the background since the various orchestral concepts had been under discussion for some time, reach a boiling point when Greg undertakes an independent, in-depth financial analysis of the proposed orchestral tour. He comes to the conclusion that such a full-fledged tour could potentially drive Emerson, Lake, and Palmer into insolvency, even if everything goes perfectly. Greg issues a single statement, 'Keith, Carl, and I have all worked very hard to reach this current point in our career, and this includes the many years even before Emerson, Lake, and Palmer were formed. There were many years of driving all night, sleeping in the van in brutal weather, literally surviving on bread and water. I cannot stand by and let everything go up in flames just to satisfy a whim. I cannot, in good conscience, participate in an orchestral Emerson, Lake, and Palmer project until we have an honest and realistic discussion. In the meantime, I will be focusing on my solo work, but I will always listen to what Keith and Carl have to say when it comes to our combined futures and ELP the band.' Keith withdraws from the spotlight, and there are rumors that he is fully committed and engaged with the concept and use of an orchestra for his music and any adaptations going forward. Insiders claim that fully orchestrated versions of Tarkus and The Endless Enigma, arranged by Keith and Godfrey Salmon, are ready to be recorded. Carl, never one to sit still for very long, consolidates his unreleased recorded output from 1974-1976 and to everyone's surprise – including Keith and Greg – releases a solo album in October 1976 simply titled Palmer.

Palmer

Track listing

Side 1

1. Carl Palmer - Concerto for Percussion

(Palmer, Joseph Horovitz)

Side 2

1. LA Nights

(Palmer)

2. The Enemy God Dances with the Black Spirits

(Sergei Prokofiev; arranged by Emerson, Palmer)

3. Food For Your Soul

(Palmer, Harry South)

4. Bullfrog

(Palmer, Ron Aspery, Colin Hodgkinson)

5. Close But Not Touching

(Palmer)

Carl. What else can be said to what already has been floating around? Time marches on, right? So, here we were approaching the end of 1976 and Keith and Greg's differences finally came to the forefront, and stayed there. I understood both their positions and rationale, but this was a bit more than casting a vote to break a tie or playing referee, which I'm really good at actually. There was no moving forward, they had both dug in their heels and each were utterly convinced they were right and that they would not be dissuaded from a goal or their vision, but for different reasons of course. They agreed to disagree, and walked out of the studio, there was no yelling, no name-calling...that was it.

Carl. I absolutely have no illusions regarding a single from my album, that's not the kind of writer I am. Perhaps there is music for cinematic adaptation. This is a specialist's album for those who know me and are interested in seeing what the percussive element of ELP would be like in its own compositional realm or as an arranger and producer of pieces. Personally, I think it's quite fascinating to see my contributions as a drummer and arranger stripped away from the Emerson and Lake musical frameworks, both as individuals and as a team. I think the hardcore ELP fans will be intrigued, at least I hope so.

Carl. As Chaucer said, time and tide wait for no man, and that includes ELP. I simply looked at the calendar and counted the years and months since we released Brain Salad Surgery or when we last played live, and it was startling to see it in black and white. It's been quite a long time, and while we went on hiatus when we had a resonance with the public and fans, so much has changed, really. I then looked at the material I had been gathering since 1974, saw the ELP was stuck in neutral as it were, and decided I was going to put out a solo record. It was as simple as that. I had the tracks and the contacts, more than enough actually, and the support from the record company who were eager to get anything related to ELP out in the marketplace.

Carl. I do hope, of course, that Keith and Greg can overcome their differences. Actually, let me rephrase that, I know that Keith and Greg will overcome their differences as ELP is still our priority, which we can all agree on. Both Keith and Greg had plenty of material ready, so the Palmer album won't delay or jeopardize any future ELP release. And, since I won't be touring in support of my album, at least not at the moment as I had cast such a wide net for the variety of contributors I felt I needed, I'm ready to go back into ELP mode at a moment's notice.

Carl. My percussion concerto has received the most attention, not from the
40

mainstream of course, but from the ELP faithful, which I find very gratifying. Honestly, I don't think it would have worked on the album we were recording or maybe any future ELP album really. We already had several substantial pieces planned as it was. I mean, yes, it was of sufficient quality and we could have put it on there, but it wouldn't have felt right to me. In a way, putting this on my solo album really is a better and ideal representation of me, my vision as a composer, and all the work I did.

Carl. Greg actually reached out to me after the Palmer album announcement was made, and he offered to help me with anything I needed. He had already done substantial work for me with guitar and production on Food For Your Soul, which turned out quite good. What I'm saying is, we do understand each other, and we're still talking. We'll always do that, even during the seemingly lowest of times.

Timeline Departure 7 – Following an emergency intervention by the record company and ELP's own accountants before the start of the Works, Volume 1 tour, the band agrees not to go on the road with the orchestra and starts the tour as a three-piece in June 1977. The five month tour (interrupted by a September break) tour is tremendously successful in rectifying ELP's balance sheet and recouping the generous advances that were eaten up by the unending logistics of the orchestral tour preparations and rehearsals. As the Works, Volume 1 tour is winding down, ELP release Works, Volume 2 in November. Following a short holiday break, ELP resume touring in January 1978 in support of the now duo of Works albums. At the tour's conclusion in April, ELP's financials are solidly in the black once again. In August, ELP enter the studio and rumors are that they are, once again, recording with an orchestra in Paris. In November, ELP release Works, Volume 3; The Gambler and Canario are released as singles, but do not chart.

Works, Volume 3

Track listing

Side 1

1. Memoirs

a. Imperial Echoes

(Arnold Safroni; arranged by Emerson)

b. Prologue/The Education of a Gentleman

(Emerson, Lake, Peter Sinfield)

c. Love at First Sight

(Emerson, Peter Sinfield)

d. Letters from the Front

(Emerson, Lake, Peter Sinfield)

e. Honourable Company (A March)

(Emerson)

Side 2

1. The Gambler

(Emerson, Lake, Peter Sinfield)

2. For You

(Lake, Peter Sinfield)

3. Marche Militaire

(Franz Schubert; arranged by Palmer)

4. Bach Before the Mast

(George Malcolm; arranged by Emerson)

5. Canario

(Joaquin Rodrigo; arranged by Emerson, Lake, Palmer)

Keith. The past two or three years have been a bit wild, to say the least. We went from a very low point, the lowest you can imagine, when we had to drop the orchestra before the Works [Volume] 1 tour even started. I can't explain how demoralizing it was; it was absolutely crushing to us and the orchestra members. After all that work and expense and looking forward to presenting our material with accompaniment from truly the finest orchestra you could imagine...nothing.

But at the conclusion of the Works [Volumes] 1 and 2 tours, we had the record company's faith in us restored and the band's internal tensions subsided as well. It was wonderful that we could use an orchestra once again for [Works] Volume 3. While we had what I could call a successful reemerging, I think the record company wanted to be a bit more cautious; we still are a band out of time, as it were. I'm convinced that it would have been magnificent with the orchestra, it would have been the rock and roll spectacle of the year; I have no doubt about that. But…facts and figures are stubborn.

Greg. While the Works [Volume] 1 and 2 albums may not have been the sellers we had hoped they would be, they have reestablished us following our lengthy hiatus; thanks to the two tours as well of course. The record company and our accountants just pummeled us with facts, figures, forecasts, warnings; we were looking at the prospect of ELP coming to an end not due to music, but due to business concerns and overwhelming obligations. At the conclusion of the Works 2 tour, the record company agreed to complete our vision of three Works albums with the 3 receiving an orchestral budget as we had for Works 1.

Carl. I don't think we were up for a double album again despite the relatively positive reaction to Works, Volume 1. For Volume 3 we have a concept piece with the Memoirs suite, and then have several band pieces as well as individual pieces; the same approach. Volume 3 is pared down Volume 1, beyond just being a single album. With Memoirs being the Pirates of 3, The Gambler and Canario being Fanfare [editor – Fanfare for the Common Man] and the bookends to the individual pieces from the three of us, rather than giving each one of us an entire side; it's all a bit more digestible.

Keith. Memoirs is very piano heavy, so I felt I just picked up where I left off with my Piano Concerto [editor – Piano Concerto, No. 1, from Works, Volume 1] and simply kept going as far as coming up with orchestral arrangements with Godfrey [editor – Godfrey Salmon, ELP orchestra conductor]. I was subconsciously taking the Tarkus approach where I had a variation of The March [editor – Honourable Company (A March)] start the piece, and then end with it, similar to what we did with Eruption. As rehearsals went on, it was a bit too predictable, too obvious; so I did a pared down arrangement of the Safroni [editor – Arnold Safroni, UK composer and writer] piece which, in addition to the wonderful and relatable title, works well on piano despite it being well known as a march; I used it as an introduction to Memoirs' Prologue segment. I initially had some doubts that it might be too obvious, almost like using Rule Britannia or the Colonel Bogey March which would have been rather gross.

Greg. Despite changes in the musical climate and culture, it was reassuring to have the record company's backing once again. They very easily could have said look, a rock band and orchestra with this seemingly pro-British sentiment in the midst of strikes, political tension, and national malaise, it's not going to work. We had to be realistic and flexible too, of course. Works 1 was a huge undertaking, and while we dodged a disaster, we kept our demands in check and were able to do Works 3 with the mindset of Works 1 but not the scope. We certainly didn't want another unwieldy behemoth, but we wanted Works 3 to be an identifiable part of what we'll look back on as our Works era, which is why we also kept the same austere approach with the Volume 3 cover in gray this time.

Carl. It's rare that when an artist's vision is interrupted that it actually is improved upon. When we embarked on the greater Works concept, we envisioned Volume 1 as the cornerstone upon which we would tour with the orchestra. We would then have a concert filmed at one of the larger venues, and we would then have a live album as well, probably the soundtrack to the movie. But when the orchestra was withdrawn and Volume 2 was put together to set the books straight – which it did because, let's be totally honest here, they were all tracks ready to go – we had the opportunity to come up with a new plot we hadn't considered with Volume 3. There's a chance we could do a one off with an orchestra and present the complete Works project as conceived, but first we'll tour in support of 3.

Keith. It was heartening to see Greg and Peter work together again after the stress of Works 1, although in this case it was Greg helping Peter rather than Peter helping Greg. After all they've been through and what we've been through going

45

back to Brain Salad Surgery, there is so much history and success that it was worth the effort to sustain this, to work through it.

Greg. I see For You very much as a sister song to C'est la Vie, both being these kind of dramatic romance tales, acoustically based but still distinct; they work very well with the orchestral enhancement. It's interesting how this happens as a composer and you can see it with the others as well. Keith's touches with Tiger in a Spotlight and The Gambler have some similarities, as do Carl's pieces Marche Militaire and the Bach piece [editor – Two Part Invention in D-Minor] as well as his other pieces Food For Your Soul and Close But Not Touching. I'm not sure why they didn't consider releasing For You as a single instead of the others, it could have worked.

Carl. Once we've completed the cycle with Volume 3 and move on, I will look back upon the Works era very fondly; it could have gone to the dogs very easily. It was a tremendous amount of work, but to see the scope of the material, the individual pieces and then the band pieces fusing and showcasing the individual strengths as one, it shows the unique and real depth of ELP.

Timeline Departure 8 – Shortly after disbanding in late 1979, ELP announce they are regrouping in early 1981 after they win a Grammy Award for their cover of Peter Gunn and are basking in the success and recognition of their In Concert album and the chart-topping performance of Peter Gunn in the Netherlands and Belgium.

For the 1980 23rd Grammy Awards, ELP win in the category Best Rock Instrumental Performance for their live interpretation of Henry Mancini's classic Peter Gunn taken from 1979's In Concert live album, narrowly beating out The Police's Regatta De Blanc. Peter Gunn had also been selected as the lead off track on a 1980 European compilation album titled Imported by Ariola, which also featured artists such as Stevie Wonder, Diana Ross, and Lou Reed. When In Concert also becomes ELP's highest charting album ever in the Netherlands (NL #3), Peter Gunn takes off not only in the Netherlands reaching a surprising NL #2 and staying on the charts for 13 weeks, but also in neighboring Belgium, topping out at BE #16 and maintaining a chart presence for five weeks. The unexpected chart success of In Concert and Peter Gunn, followed by the even greater unexpected and surprising Grammy win, prompts ELP to reconvene.

Keith. A Grammy for ELP; it certainly sounds odd. [Pause] Well, I really don't know how...well, I do know how, but it certainly is a shock, a pleasant shock, I think. When I first heard rumors that we were nominated, I figured it was either a joke, or they were mocking us following our break-up. Nothing surprises me anymore when it comes to how the press treats ELP. Then, I found out that we really had been nominated and we were in a category that really fit ELP well, against some very popular artists, The Police, The Pretenders...and then, yeah, we won. At first I felt that it was a bit of a back-handed compliment, after all our original works, we get recognition for doing a cover, but, what do you do. Other than fan or magazine polls, ELP never won much, but something like this, from the industry, I'm still quite astonished.

Greg. Some people are probably surprised, but ELP is not a complete stranger to Grammy nominations, even before winning this year. I believe we were nominated for best new artist and then for best instrumental performance with Pictures at an Exhibition. Considering how we were always tortured by the critics, and that we were nominated following our break-up in 1979, it seemed like mockery done in extremely bad taste. But, then the reality hit that this was truly happening, and that we won, much to their horrors I'm sure. I thought after being in rock and roll for over 10 years that I had learned to read between the lines, but somebody threw out the script with this, or maybe somebody didn't follow orders. ELP has done some amazing instrumentals that were easily just as worthy as Peter Gunn, if not more so, but sometimes it all just comes down to timing. Who knows, really? I'm very proud of our performance, Keith's interpretation and synth arrangement is both brilliantly modern and gracious to the original.

Carl. When it comes to note density on ELP recordings, this [editor - Peter Gunn] probably ranks near the bottom, but...when something works, it works, exactly as it's worked for Henry Mancini and all the way to ELP for over 20 years. We were also quite fortunate that all those wonderful, moody brass arrangements lend themselves to the capabilities of modern synthesizers in the hands of someone like Keith.

Keith. What's the old saying? Never say never...ever, right? I was about to embark on scoring a movie for Dario Argento [editor – Italian producer, director, and screenwriter], a sort of a companion or follow-up to his movie Suspiria, when I got the call. I thought to myself, hang on now, let's go over a couple of things. I just left ELP with a slightly bad taste in the mouth, but it was about the situation we were thrust in, not with Greg and Carl. And now I'm being offered to work with a budget where I can get whatever I reasonably need to fill any musical role, you know? Need a jazz singer? No problem, there you are. Need a great French horn player? No problem. But, it just reeks of...routine, no spontaneity. Momentum or inertia can happen at the most unexpected times.

Greg. Shortly after ELP's official disbanding, I started writing and recording a large amount of material, very much guitar oriented songs. I was, of course, consciously stepping away from the ELP framework as a dedicated guitar player once again. But, I always came back to thinking, how would Keith voice these chords, what input what Carl provide on the arrangement, suggesting a break here, a bridge there, or something...it's what I'm used to, it's what I did, and what we did for 10 years. And you know, all of sudden having this burst of success and profile, the timing is a bit unusual.

Carl. After ELP disbanded I had properly advertised and was looking for a more conventional band sound; I quite enjoy bands like the Police, you know, ironically you could now say. But anyway, I was going through all the audition tapes, hundreds of them, and I was very close to making my final decision; interestingly enough, I had chosen mostly Americans. When management called I thought, the first thing I'm going to do is call Keith and Greg. After all, we couldn't agree on anything for a farewell tour in 1979, but success, even delayed, can be a tremendous motivator and salve for a bad experience.

Keith. It's our intention to do a very low-key, European-only tour, not a comeback as such and certainly no big production. We'll consider it a sort of a toe in the water approach, no America this time. Of course we'd like to hit the UK, we'll be happy if they'll have us. I do have quite a bit of music to share with Greg and Carl that falls within the ELP style, as it is. It certainly won't fit in with what's in vogue now, so we'll have to see if the interest is still there.

Greg. Acceptance of any kind is a wonderful thing if it occurs naturally, mass acceptance even more so. While Peter Gunn is not our composition, it is a wonderful, legendary piece of music that we tackled with great skill and respect, if I say so myself. Funnily enough, it was just brought to my attention that Peter Gunn has already outperformed Lucky Man in both Holland and Belgium...interesting bookends in the band's career one might say...or maybe not a bookend.

Carl. It was Greg's suggestion to incorporate Peter Gunn in our Works' tour setlist. It was a fresh idea and approach, and with the sound he was getting on the 8-string Alembic bass, it projected magnificently. We did learn one thing from our extended break before the Works project, or projects if you will. That being, if we

49

have any intent or notion of reforming, the longer we wait the less enthusiastic or broad the response will be and will have an effect on our long term presence; it's a reality. We've experienced that pain once before, and we certainly don't want to do so again.

Keith. We've toured Holland before, but I had forgotten just how well ELP had been received there when we started out. We had a particularly memorable concert in Rotterdam in 1974 I believe it was, where we went down exceptionally well; a classic ELP riot as we called it. Although, knowing some of the classically influenced bands that have come out of Holland, it's not a complete surprise that ELP would strike a chord there. Focus [editor – Dutch progressive rock band] were a very good band, and of course I'm very familiar with Rick van der Linden of Ekseption [editor - Ekseption is a Dutch progressive rock band anchored by classically trained keyboardist Rick; Keith and Rick co-wrote a track on Ekseption's album 5, titled For Example / For Sure].

Greg. When Peter Gunn started climbing the charts in Holland, I was reminded that excepting England, Holland was the only other country where our first five records went top-10, pretty astonishing really. I do remember that we shared a bill with the Dutch band Focus for the [editor – 1972] Melody Maker Poll Awards Concert at the legendary Oval Cricket Ground. Another interesting quasi ELP-Dutch connection if you will, is that C'est la Vie actually was a hit in South Africa in 1977, I believe it went top 20 or so [editor – SA #14].

Carl. Wherever you experience a spike in popularity or have a bit of profile, you want to react appropriately and create, continue, or rekindle some kind of long-term legacy beyond record sales for live performance. We have had chart success in Holland before, but In Concert has charted higher than any of our previous albums, that includes both studio and live releases. Considering where ELP was at the time, this is a tremendous surprise. You know, you can study sales trends, radio reports, and work like mad to get some recognition, and then other times it just takes off on its own. I mean, we can't seem to get arrested in France going on ten years now, but then in Holland there's a substantial recognition of

ELP; one never knows for sure how these things happen or play out.

Timeline Departure 9 – Keith is not injured in a motorcycle crash in June of 1987 when ELP reconvenes and continues with rehearsals after being invited as a special guest for a series of three shows at the Out in the Green concert series held in West Germany and Switzerland in July of that year. Barclay James Harvest, Status Quo, and Kansas perform with ELP on their three dates.

Keith. The phone call came at just the right time for all three of us, unexpectedly; sometimes it just works out that way. Things kind of turned sour with Cozy [editor – Cozy Powell, drummer] as our tour was coming to an end, which was a shame, really, as he is a lovely guy even though he's rightfully known as a bit of a wildman. And, of course, we had completely burned through the advance for the second album on production for the first tour; we are genuine creatures of habit. Although I must say, it was great fun and while attendance in some areas was spotty, some of the crowds were fantastic. For some shows we had two encores a night, you know, it can't get much better than that. But when we played our last show in I think it was Arizona [editor – state in the southwestern United States], Cozy sped off in a cloud of dust on one of his racing motorcycles.

Greg. Emerson, Lake, and Powell suffered through terrible management, absolutely dreadful. We tried to tell them repeatedly that it's not 1973, it's 1986, but they wouldn't listen. What I'm saying is that the expectations were not realistic, no matter how enthusiastic you are. While we had more than acceptable sales, especially in Canada where the album went Gold, and some video and chart exposure with Touch and Go in the US [editor – US #60], it just fizzled out much quicker than we would have liked. There were some plans to record a second album in Holland with Alan Parsons, but, nothing was formally scheduled and there were some questions on finances. But, we then received a nice phone call.

Carl. The Astra record [editor – Asia's third studio album] back in 1985 was just endless work, writing, recording, mixing, finding the right producer. Time got away from us and opportunity literally passed us by. We did a video [editor – Go, Astra's leadoff single] but then management withdrew support when the record didn't take off like the first record. They were holding us to an impossible standard, even if it was our own. It had been three years since the Asia debut and then basically two years of silence from Asia after the Alpha album. A world tour had been planned for early 1986, and when that support got pulled, the band just collapsed, I don't know how else to describe it.

Carl. I think John [editor – John Wetton, bassist and lead vocalist for Asia] was a bit dismayed with it all, all the work on Astra, it led nowhere. Perhaps he was still upset about the whole Asia in Asia matter [editor – a limited, but high-profile 1983 Asia tour of Japan with Greg Lake temporarily replacing John], but he had some urgent personal matters to attend to as well. Of course, we all had been dealing with the tension between Steve [editor – Steve Howe, Asia guitarist] and John, and then Geoff [editor – Geoff Downes, Asia keyboardist] had mountains of work to do to help Mandy [editor – Mandy Meyer, Asia guitarist, replacement for Steve Howe] properly get up to speed. I'd been hearing bits and pieces of news that things weren't going that well with Cozy and that he abruptly left Keith and Greg, and so here we are. For a short time after John left, I thought I could perhaps salvage Asia. I'd heard of a talented chap named Robert Berry from my manager Brian Lane. Robert is an American, and is quite ambitious as well as a talented multi-instrumentalist. In mid or late 1986 I formally reached out to him about joining Asia, but time marches on you know. We then received the offer from the Out in the Green people and then ELP took precedence once again. The last I heard is that Robert may be doing something with a reconfigured GTR with Steve Howe.

Keith. Rehearsals were going well, and as we were starting production planning and rehearsals I had a bit of a scare on my motorcycle while heading home. I then decided: no more and I started driving my car once again. I almost found out the hard way that it's not like it was 15 years ago, it's just too crowded anymore.

Greg. We are willing to do what we need to do to get back in the public eye, just like we did with Cozy in North America. True, it wasn't ELP proper, but the fact is that we could be Emerson, Lake, and Powell because there was an Emerson, Lake, and Palmer. It's the hard truth, there's no denying it, I mean, look at the setlist.

We did three songs from the Emerson, Lake, and Powell album and 12 or 13 were from the Emerson, Lake, and Palmer catalog. It had been eight years since the ELP catalog had been played live; it was very rewarding to see the reactions from the audience. And, since we're only playing in Germany and Switzerland to start out with, where ELP always has had a good following, we're hopeful for a good response. I'm hearing that Italy is a good possibility as well.

Carl. It's very important that we just take some short strides before any big plans are made. Music is different, music tastes are different, radio is different, and now you have the video medium to contend with. Certainly, some people know who we are, we haven't been out of the spotlight for 20 years, but we don't want to be rash and we want to have a plan. I know Keith has plenty of music, that's never a problem. I just want to make sure we've gotten over the various bumps we've all had, Keith and Greg dealing with Cozy's sudden departure and some management issues, myself dealing with Asia falling apart. I'm looking forward to some long-lasting stability once again.

Timeline Departure 10 – The Black Moon album is never recorded.

In late 1991, as the sessions for the planned Black Moon studio album were about to commence, producer Mark Mancina bows out to accept a lucrative movie soundtrack offer. Keith, Greg, and Carl cannot agree on another producer as Keith and Carl are unwilling to cede the producer's chair solely to Greg. The sessions eventually are canceled, and the ELP reunion drifts apart.

Keith. We started out not with an ELP reunion at the forefront, but with the very best of intentions with an offer to work on a movie soundtrack from an old friend in the business, Phil Carson. It seemed rather logical, with my experience and our combined histories as well as the track record of ELP. The soundtrack idea was positively received by all; it then became a proposal for an album which turned into an idea for a proper, full-fledged reunion. Perhaps we moved a bit too quickly, but the dreaded production question reared its head again. While I don't want to say too much, we simply couldn't agree once Mark Mancina went off to greener pastures, he can't be blamed at all as he received a once in a lifetime offer.

Greg. Once the proposal for an album was floated, Keith and I brought material we had been working on. It is true, we composed some material together, all three of us actually. But the majority came from Keith and I, songs from other projects, or our solo material. What I'm saying is that a good portion of the music that was supposed to be part of the ELP reunion was already in a completed, written state.

Carl. I had been asked by Geoff Downes [editor – Asia keyboardist] to complete some drum tracks for a new Asia album, as both ELP and Asia were in London at the time. Geoff is still very committed to Asia, and while I was committed to the ELP reunion, I admired his enthusiasm and perseverance. But then, as is now known, Mark [editor – Mark Mancina, producer, composer, and arranger] then suddenly asked to excuse himself from the project. We then found ourselves in our Love Beach mode, which meant a lot of discussions and not much compromising. This unfortunately led to very little progress, and eventually the project came to a halt.

Keith. I thought we had some very promising material, but we didn't have an extended suite of any kind. That is kind of what would be expected from an ELP reunion, I would think, or at least a thoroughly proper and genuine ELP reunion. It wasn't a deal breaker for any of us though. But even so, I still felt that the tracks we had were of significant quality for the creation of a very strong, ELP identifiable record. You know, we had the Hammond, some instrumentals, a solo piano piece; Greg had some nice acoustic songs. But, for all the reasons things fall by the wayside, this did. I have plenty of material, enough for a solo CD I'm sure, and after working with The Best [editor – an English-American supergroup consisting of Keith, John Entwistle/The Who, Joe Walsh/The Eagles, Jeff 'Skunk' Baxter/Steely Dan and the Doobie Brothers as the main members that briefly toured Japan], while it was quite limited, it reaffirmed my confidence as a writer and performer after being on the sidelines for a few years.

Greg. I knew Carl had been working with Geoff [editor – Geoff Downes, Asia keyboardist] when the ELP reunion started gathering momentum, and that was totally fine, we understood that Carl is integral to both bands. I, too, received a call from Geoff when he heard the ELP reunion fell apart, asking me what my plans were. Geoff and I worked together quite recently on a project called Ride the Tiger when he wanted to take a break from Asia. We shopped around several songs, but couldn't get a deal at the time. Since then, Geoff was planning to use one song for the new Asia album, and I was planning on using one or two songs for the ELP reunion album albeit one with different music and one a different arrangement or interpretation as we were arranging the tracks for the album. I'm not sure where all this will lead as I hear Geoff has a new singer in mind. The time spent writing, recording, and delving into the world of MIDI with Geoff was enjoyable as he is truly a world-class player, composer, and arranger. It was a great experience, and it brought back some good memories from our brief, but difficult time in Asia, no detriment to Geoff of course. We ultimately didn't wind up with a lot of finished songs, maybe six or seven, but there was quite a bit of music. It also was wonderful working with Mike [editor – Mike Giles, original King

Crimson drummer] again; we confirmed the original magic was still there.

Carl. With ELP sidelined, I can now fully devote time and energy to the new Asia project. I haven't been back in the studio with Geoff since ELP splintered, and I know he's been in contact with Greg whom he worked with at length in the late '80's. I especially remember that as Geoff wasn't available for a brief Asia tour at the time, I think it was in Europe. But, anyway, I don't see Greg stepping into Asia on a full-time basis, but I can't say for sure. I don't think Geoff would ask Greg at this time, but, they have written some good material together, it's more middle-of-the-road, mainstream I would say, and they have high regard for one another as well.

Timeline Departure 11 – In the Hot Seat is never recorded.

In mid-1994, ELP are in the studio working on In the Hot Seat and discover producer Keith Olsen (previously worked with Fleetwood Mac, Foreigner, Heart, among others) is sabotaging ELP's planned reworking of The Nice's classic adaptation of the Karelia Suite [editor - by Finnish composer Jean Sibelius]. Fed up with the band being stymied at every nod towards a progressive approach, they storm out of the studio and the sessions crash to an end. Keith and Carl retire to their haunts, while Greg continues working with ELP technician Keith Wechsler and sets up shop in a different studio in the Los Angeles area. Greg completes two of his tracks that were destined for In the Hot Seat, Daddy and Heart on Ice, and releases it as a Greg Lake solo CD single in November 1994; a re-recording of I Believe in Father Christmas is also included to take advantage of the upcoming holidays. Daddy manages to capture some mainstream attention, both as a song and for the cause of missing children, but does not chart.

Keith. I'd simply had enough; I was done with it, that's it. Between the anxiety of my own physical condition and then being forced into this bizarre notion that ELP could start spitting out these neat, radio-oriented singles...it was ridiculous. I remember sitting in the studio, warming up on Lachesis or Pirates, and then having some Chicago-like ballad put in front of me, something about don't leave me. Yeah, Ok, but...no. I'm thinking, what am I doing, what are we doing? What's going on here? This is ELP, that's what.

Greg. Keith [editor – Keith Olsen, producer] is a talented and established producer...very professional, very qualified, just look at his track record. But, he just didn't understand ELP, and not many industry people do, and never will. As a result, even the three of us, with all our experience, found ourselves a bit baffled as to what was happening very slowly and subtly...it was like the frog in the boiling pot of water, you know? The final straw was when we were putting major efforts into the recording of the Karelia Suite and all of a sudden Olsen feigned incompetence and couldn't do anything right. We already had argued about ELP doing the Firebird Suite [editor – by Russian composer Igor Stravinsky], and when

58

that was rejected we suggested Karelia which was accepted by Olson, but then he did nothing with it. It was an out and out mess.

Carl. Keith and I battled through some physical challenges...and we were doing it, you know...we were persevering, it wasn't easy. But then we found out that Olsen was purposely obstructing us while pretending to be toiling away on our behalf, which was very, very disappointing. But, you know, it's what you have to expect when you're dealing with this California way of doing business.

Keith. In an odd way, maybe this was best, at least for the album we were making. I thought, as we all thought, that we had a reasonable amount of momentum after Black Moon, the album charted in several countries, we followed that up with significant amounts of touring, including places ELP had not been before. We absolutely had a great time. We then played the Royal Albert Hall as a validation for this new era of ELP, and then had the live album to document that [editor – ELP live album, Live at the Royal Albert Hall]. I mean, that's a lot of hard work to do and put a stamp on a proper comeback. But then to all of a sudden be thrust into this pop mentality? Perhaps we saved ourselves from some possible embarrassment, who knows; I don't claim to know. We do have some quality material and plenty of ideas; I'm confident we can pick up the pieces and reorganize ourselves.

Greg. Recording Daddy and Heart on Ice with Keith Wechsler was not some purposeful move away from ELP. These were two of my tracks that had some of the old ELP inspiration which I wanted to capture, and working on them without Olsen allowed me to present them as I saw fit, not through someone else. I just wanted to get them done and get them out, it just felt right to do so. Daddy was sincere and honest motivation; Heart on Ice doesn't work as some piano ballad, which is what Olsen thought, it just sounded wrong, so I brought it back to how I originally envisioned it.

Greg. The re-recording of Father Christmas was not planned or considered during the sessions with Olsen. Keith [editor – Keith Wechsler, ELP technician] is our personal, secret weapon, which made everything go quickly and smoothly in the

59

wake of tension from the sessions. He knows ELP, the material, and the technology back to front, which made this relatively easy. After we had set up shop, someone suggested that with the holidays approaching maybe adding I Believe in Father Christmas to the release would be a nice touch, and I agreed.

Carl. Sometimes it's better to step away from what looks like a possible disaster, not even a guaranteed one. Looking back on it now, we had some good tracks...but that's it, simply a collection of tracks. And then, for some reason, we started buying tracks, outside writers who were professional and talented for what they do, but it was so far removed from ELP. We were sitting around one day before a session, and we looked at each other. We asked ourselves, really? ELP needs outside writers now? No, we never did, and we won't.

Keith. I'm hopeful that this unintended break gives Carl and myself the opportunity to rest and recoup a bit more and give the band a chance to reset and evaluate what to do next after all this, I have no doubt we will do something. This may have been the unexpected event to help us refocus on what makes ELP, ELP.

Greg. I don't see this as a step towards another solo album, not at all, nor was I considering one. While these are quite obviously tracks in my style, I haven't embellished them with a Keith and Carl sound-alike nor have I gone out looking for a band, as such. They [editor – Keith and Carl] have been supportive of a cause that's dear to my heart, and this gives them a bit of time to heal, to focus on getting completely well without limitations or restrictions. We still are most definitely committed to ELP, all three of us are. If anything, I think we've come to realize we've dodged a bullet. It's given us motivation to recognize, again, what we do best and what the fans expect from us, which is the classic ELP with its epic pieces and grand concepts.

Carl. I think Greg is going to do a bit of promotion for Daddy, some regional shows and press in the northeast US. I believe he's working with some local activists for the cause, which the ELP organization totally supports. When Greg's done, and after Keith and I have spent some more time recuperating, we'll get together and discuss the band's direction. We do have material ready to go. Personally, I would like to do some touring, but we need to keep Keith's and my own health and well-being in mind. Perhaps we can find another legacy artist, another act from our era, that we can open for, a full set might be too much right now. Maybe a co-headlining tour would work, and then we can consider working on some new music.

Timeline Departure 11A – In the Hot Seat is recorded and released, but with a slightly modified tracklist.

In September 1994 ELP release In the Hot Seat, their ninth studio album, produced by industry stalwart Keith Olsen (previously worked with Fleetwood Mac, Foreigner, Heart, among others). In the Hot Seat is the third album of ELP's 1990's reincarnation following the studio album Black Moon and aptly titled Live at the Royal Albert Hall. While the album has some minor progressive tendencies, the combination of pressure from Victory Records to deliver an album with commercial potential and Keith and Carl managing their respective health challenges, it turns out to be far from the slab of epic work ELP fans were hoping for. The album manages a brief chart appearance in Japan before disappearing from view everywhere, which is what ELP does as Keith and Carl focus on their health and the floundering Victory Records struggles to remain afloat. Shortly after the album's release and in the wake of the usual vitriolic reviews, ELP cancel their planned North American and Japanese tours. Daddy is released as a single, but does not chart.

In the Hot Seat

Track listing

1. Hand of Truth

(Emerson, Lake)

2. Daddy

(Lake)

3. One by One

(Emerson, Lake, Keith Olsen)

4. Heart on Ice

(Lake, Keith Olsen)

5. Hammer It Out

(Emerson)

6. Man in the Long Black Coat

(Bob Dylan)

7. Change

(Emerson, Lake, Keith Olsen)

8. Intermezzo, from the Karelia Suite

(Jean Sibelius, arranged by Emerson, Lake, Palmer)

9. Gone Too Soon

(Lake, Keith Wechsler)

10. Street War

(Emerson, Lake)

Emerson. This album was a mighty struggle, not only were we fighting Victory Records, but Carl and I were doing our best to perform and deliver at the level we and our fans have been accustomed to. When the record company and Olsen [editor – Keith Olsen, producer] started shoving outside songs and writers our way, we'd had enough and put our foot down.

Greg. As is the case with most any organization, the top level is disconnected from the middle which handles all the day to day matters. We will always have a good relationship with Phil Carson [editor – CEO Victory Records] due to our history, but the grief we were getting from mid-level management was absurd. I mean, telling us we needed a certain snare sound, or that we had to work with this and that outside writer to try and get airplay, or a hit.

Carl. You only have so much energy to deal with the matters at hand, right? And you can only be pushed so much before you push back, which is what we did. We pushed back and said no to outside writers, excepting Olsen who was with us in the studio, and we held him accountable for ensuring the Karelia [editor - Intermezzo from the Karelia Suite by Jean Sibelius] tape made its way to Trevor Rabin [editor – Yes guitarist and producer]. We had to call on Phil [editor – Phil Carson] a few times as a gentle reminder, we could use that leverage because of our history with him and since Yes was with Victory Records at the time as well. Working with professionals shouldn't be that hard, but it was exhausting...very, very draining.

Keith. When I look back, I thought it was interesting that we found ourselves in a situation where recording a track that was part of ELP's pre-history no longer had the pushback that it would have had in the '70's, you know? I mean, it was a different era for the band, which shows how the situation at hand can dictate one's path and then change later. We were running like mad with this album, just not to fall behind or to let it fall to pieces. It took a lot of pressure, but we finally got Olsen to do what he needed to do to finish up Karelia. The Firebird Suite [editor – by Russian composer Igor Stravinsky] is a wonderful piece of music and was also considered, but when we thought about it and discussed it in more detail, it's so closely associated with Yes, perhaps too closely for ELP to use it as well. We thought it better to do something that at least is directly and only related to ELP's history.

Greg. The record company kept trying to ram outside, generic tracks down our throats, that's all I really want to say. We know what our fans are looking for, and while we unfortunately couldn't provide an epic ELP piece for a variety of reasons, at least we could give them a trademark piano piece by Keith instead of some non-descript ballad. That would be an honest effort to at least try and give the album some ELP-like identity.

Carl. Ensconced in Olsen's Goodnight LA studio, which is a very nice facility actually, we found ourselves dealing with very nice individuals who thought they understood ELP and had some grand insight as to what we needed to do or what we were doing wrong, but the reality is they knew nothing of our history, absolutely nothing. They were interested in pushing product, professional bean counters, period. What's the old saying? The bean counter knows the cost of everything, but the value of nothing.

Chapter One

Winter's Light, 1975

Emerson, Lake, and Palmer

The Alternate History

1975-2000

Following the August 1974 release of their triple live album Welcome Back My Friends to the Show That Never Ends, ELP agree to go on an extended break to recharge and revive their personal lives and professional energies. In late 1974, Greg and his former King Crimson bandmate and lyricist Peter Sinfield get together and compose the acoustically-centered, but orchestral-enhanced I Believe in Father Christmas which Greg shares with Keith; Greg believes it is destined to be an ELP track. Having recorded and missed the Christmas 1974 deadline to release the track, by mid-1975 there is interest and preparation from the record company to release it as a Greg solo track for the upcoming Holiday season. However, situations and opportunities present themselves upon which management convinces the band to put out an album with I Believe in Father Christmas as the cornerstone track, despite the band desperately clamoring for a break. Not wishing to fray nerves, the band's management scrapes together various tracks from the band's archives to gather enough material for an album. In November 1975, ELP release the single album Winter's Light; I Believe in Father Christmas is released as a single and becomes a smash hit UK #2. Tiger in a Spotlight and Oh, My Father are also released as singles, but do not chart.

Immediately following Winter's Light's release, the band does not go on a grand, expansive tour as they've done in the past, rather they only commit to select radio and TV shows in Europe and the US to promote I Believe in Father Christmas.

Winter's Light

Track listing

Side 1

1. I Believe in Father Christmas

(Lake, Peter Sinfield)

2. Brain Salad Surgery

(Emerson, Lake, Peter Sinfield)

3. Tiger in a Spotlight

(Emerson, Lake, Palmer, Peter Sinfield)

4. Prelude and Fugue

(Friedrich Gulda; arranged by Emerson)

5. Bo Diddley

(Grant Green, John Patton; arranged by Emerson, Lake, Palmer)

Side 2

1. Barrelhouse Shakedown

(Emerson)

2. When the Apple Blossoms Bloom in the Windmills of Your Mind, I'll Be Your Valentine

(Emerson, Lake, Palmer)

3. Oh, My Father

(Lake)

4. Two Part Invention in D-minor

(Johann S. Bach; arranged by Palmer)

5. Lifeline

(Palmer, Harry South)

Keith. Well, Gregory hits the jackpot again, right? I'm sorry, I meant ELP [laughs]. When he first played the acoustic guitar theme [editor – from I Believe in Father Christmas] for me, the Prokofiev [editor – Sergei Prokofiev, Russian composer] theme [editor – from Lieutenant Kije] just flew out of me. I admit it gave me absolute chills hearing it in its completed state. We really, really thought about taking a long break and reevaluating ELP's direction. But, I have to tell you about a brief trip I took to Paris in 1973 or 1974. I was checking out all of these marvelous little jazz clubs and I came upon Jacques Loussier [editor – French pianist and composer] who just has this wonderful way of incorporating and blending classical and jazz, simply brilliant. Carl and I are very familiar with him. While our conversation was personal, I will say it was hugely impactful in that it helped me recognize what we all have with ELP, and what I have. I don't want to throw it away on a solo venture or imposing a solo vision on the band. I hope there will be time for that in the future should our schedule slow down, like it has now, somewhat.

Greg. Had it not been for Phil Carson [editor – Atlantic Records executive] being out of the country on holiday with his return flight delayed and the local phone service cut for a week due to inclement weather, this [editor – I Believe in Father Christmas] very well could have been my solo single. With the rush and success of

ELP it's been very tempting to take a break and maybe put out a solo album, or multiple solo albums. This is something that has been talked about for Keith and me since Trilogy or right before Brain Salad Surgery or so. But, we all realize the group just has too much to offer. Plus, we always seem to find out that as soon as we come up with something for one of our possible solo albums; it simply works too well in a band setting.

Carl. Well, it's a fantastic song, and the public seems to agree, so what else can you say? Is it representative of ELP? In the context of an album, sure, it is Greg the minstrel at work per usual amongst a collection of ELP tracks, that being collaborative performance. I know in the past when considering Still You Turn Me On as a single there was a concern that it wasn't representative of the band as a whole, but circumstances were certainly different then. Also, with Keith's substantial input on the Prokofiev theme, and being on an ELP album, we are being honest with ourselves and the fans that this is ELP.

Keith. Yes, it's true; it's certainly not a secret that there were talks on-and-off about solo albums from both myself and Greg, quite serious talks actually. I'm not so sure about Carl or what he preferred, but he doesn't slow down and he always has some side projects in the works. The record company was certainly interested in us as solo artists considering the profile we had created with ELP. But, you know, I'm in a band, a good band. And when I recall and see all the vitriol spewed our way over the years, I figured it's because we were too good, so why not continue to work with the band because we really are that good.

Greg. It was Keith's suggestion, and quite a good one, to incorporate the Prokofiev theme with Father Christmas. Even if I had been pressured for a solo single, that made it, in my opinion, destined to be an ELP track. It is one of the band's hallmarks, you know, this classical influence. ELP is very fortunate to maintain a position of relative prominence for five years running now.

Carl. ELP continues to have very, very good fortune, and good songs of course. You need both really in this business, maybe good fortune even more so. I hear plenty of aspiring bands that are good musicians, they have good material, but

69

they're missing an ingredient. It might be their management, getting the right ears to hear them. Are they sufficiently dynamic in a live setting? Although, that might not be as important now as it was in the 1960's, but it doesn't hurt. Additionally, so many bands put years of work into their first record and when the time comes for a follow-up, the well's run dry. One mustn't overlook the need and ability to keep creating quality material, even in the wake of success.

Keith. Many artists release a Christmas track because, if you have any kind of profile, it's bound to get some attention, eventually. And, if you're lucky it will catch on and keep reappearing for many years to come. Also, there are so many well-known and recognizable Christmas songs out there for the taking, these are songs immediately recognized, internationally. So, I don't think some of the critics are being very fair with us once again, as usual. ELP is not unfamiliar with adapting and rearranging pieces, but Greg's piece is an original piece of music and is enhanced by the Prokofiev line. I might even explore doing a Christmas record of my own some day.

Greg. To be working with Pete again and coming up with Father Christmas has been extremely energizing and encouraging. I think his scope as a lyricist will eventually broaden to more pop or mainstream appeal, not necessarily with ELP; maybe with others that will come to recognize his obvious talent. That's never a bad thing of course.

Carl. Winter's Light is certainly an Emerson, Lake, and Palmer album, but it is a bit light on the Emerson, Lake, and Palmer tracks as some have pointed out. Sure, Tiger in a Spotlight and Brain Salad Surgery are band tracks, but those had been in the bin since 1972 or 1973. We actually had recorded and kept Tiger in a Spotlight in reserve in case Keith and Ginestera [editor – Alberto Ginestera, Argentinian composer of Toccata that appeared on ELP's Brain Salad Surgery album] couldn't come to an agreement for ELP to release the Toccata. But I understand, or I have come to understand, that it is difficult as an artist to sometimes play what is called a long game, when you want to do something [loudly] RIGHT NOW! [Laughs] Being in ELP is like being in the army, so I've heard. So, we hurry up, and then we wait and wait, and then we go like mad again.

Keith. Yeah, I know we'll get slagged on by the press even more than usual and maybe by some ELP purists claiming that we cobbled together an album for the sake of Father Christmas, and that the signature, ELP-style lengthy, grandiose track is missing. I can see their point, certainly. There are older tracks, some forgotten tracks, and maybe even some that sound just like some jamming. But, we were contemplating a break of sorts anyway following the latest back-breaking tour supporting Brain Salad Surgery. Did we want to step away? After three or four years of non-stop touring and recording, and even longer if you consider we were all busy before ELP, we very much needed to. This is all true, but we also didn't want to lose our profile, this was a compromise without surrendering our integrity. Besides, it's difficult to be very down when the single is doing so well, right?

Keith. I think my only wish, or regret, is that the record company could have chosen a slightly better album title. It's a bit, I think one could say, Cliff Richard'ish [laughs], no knock on Cliff of course who truly is a British icon. I'm sure a casual survey of our fans taken at the local grocery store or airport wouldn't think the title is something they've come to expect from ELP as well, far from it probably. Every high profile band seems to have at least one naff album title in the catalog, hopefully this was ours.

Keith. It shouldn't come as too much of a surprise that I would have composed a piece like Barrelhouse Shakedown, as I truly do love ragtime piano. For anyone that has heard my piano improvisations, I would hope that they see the connection, or the influence. While obviously seen as an American art form, our American fans might not realize that we have some great ragtime players in the UK. The legendary Winifred Atwell of course is amazing, as is Dill Jones who has a great jazz touch.

Greg. All of us were looking forward to a break, a well-deserved one. But, nothing compares to putting out a quality record, which I believe we have, even beyond the single. The record company is confident that Father Christmas will become part of the Christmas music canon as time goes on; wouldn't that be nice? Some of our usual critics haven't gone for the throat just yet; maybe they haven't heard the whole album.

Carl. Well, I personally think we fell a bit short on delivering another vintage ELP album. We have had an amazing run, and Winter's Light [editor – Carl mumbling, "Let alone the daft title"] is really and rightfully focused around Greg's song and some odds and sods, mind you, they're pretty good odds and sods. But, yes, it is missing that grand, extended musical statement that ELP has become known for.

Carl. I actually caught some stick from a punter about Bo Diddley, not unexpectedly. Yes, of course we know it was by Big John Patton [editor – the piece is called The Yodel written by Grant Green and Big John Patton]. At the end of the day it's just a fun tune, and people get to hear Greg play more electric guitar than usual. Interestingly, I'm hearing Keith's boogie-woogie piano skills might be getting attention in Italy, who would have thought that the land of Michelangelo would be enamored by Keith's beer-breath saloon piano! No, but seriously, the Italians have always been great to ELP, and we love playing there.

Keith. While I miss the excitement of the big tours and production, it's amazing to relax a bit. As mentioned before, we were in desperate need of a break, as a band and as individuals. Mind you, TV's not always all that easy, since it's a bit sparse there's no hiding behind a wall of volume, so it needs to be on, if you know what I mean. But, one gets the feeling that it is a bit like we're on holiday of sorts, except we're traveling quite light [laughs]. But seriously, this is the perfect way to allow us to recharge our batteries yet remain engaged with ELP.

Greg. The reaction to Father Christmas has been staggering, not so much in the USA despite the promotion we're doing, but in the UK, it has been amazing. I think it's been absolutely great to have connected with our UK fan base, or reconnected if you will. Following ELP's first several albums, it seems that we had a primary focus on the USA with our AOR success and sales totals, which followed with the heavy touring we did there. It is of course, as a European band, the market you want to crack by virtue of its massive scale and size, so I'm glad we could refocus a bit on our home country.

Carl. I'm not one for taking a break and such, one has to strike, and keep striking, while the iron is hot as inactivity does not bode well ever. Someone please prove me wrong. But, yeah, the reaction to the single has been great, it is quite nice to be treated like royalty for a five minute TV appearance and not having the headache or worry of tracking 10 tons of equipment from town to town. There's the constant worrying about thievery, equipment breaking down, scavenging for spare parts, the road crew having bouts of madness. There are many stressful concerns with every large-scale tour, and we tend to be very hands on as we've absorbed some hard-earned lessons, as most successful musicians have. The only thing that is annoying is the dreadfully small radio stations we wind up visiting on occasion. But either way, I show up with a triangle and tambourine, [laughing] no need to worry about a solo this time folks.

Keith. Despite Winter's Light being a spontaneous release, but not really a completely spontaneous recording obviously, I am happy that it contains all the elements that one could say make up an ELP album but not in a totally extravagant way, you know? With Father Christmas' mainstream success perhaps that will expose the band to a segment that just knows about ELP being a performer of epic suites, especially when they see the true variety of shorter songs on the album done in the unique ELP style.

Greg. There is a bit of an imbalance on the record if you really, really wanted to do some fault finding. I will grant the critics that, but only insofar as that there are many instrumental pieces, which is not unusual at all for ELP. To support that, I mean, just look at Side Two of the first album, right? You would think that we have learned by now to ignore the critics and just listen to the fans.

Carl. Lifeline is the result of working with the great jazz pianist Harry South who's more than a bit of a legend in England. You wonder why I worked with him and not Phil Seaman [editor – renowned British jazz drummer] as well? Well, there's only room for one drummer in a band, usually. He [editor - Harry South] is not only a great technician, but a very inventive and bountiful composer in his own right. It was great to have his help and skills with the vibraphone arrangement, and as such I've already booked some more time in the future to work with him.

Following the 1975 holiday season and promotional tour for Winter's Light (or more accurately, I Believe In Father Christmas) through January 1976, ELP reconvene at Manticore headquarters in March. Keith, Greg, Carl, and manager Stewart Young sequester themselves there for three weeks. Despite the post-impact of I Believe in Father Christmas' performance on the charts and what seems to have been a condensed, but very successful tour, there is no contact, no interviews are granted. At the end of those three weeks, Stewart calls a press conference that lasts a mere 10 minutes.

Keith. [Reserved] Well, I've been told that more of the same is wanted? That's what I've been told.

Greg. Over the years, the others have trusted me in the production chair and with certain business matters because it worked. It was obvious to our inner circle how and why it worked, and we have become like family. Sometimes you argue, sometimes there is no obvious right or clear path. Sometimes people need to be reined in, and sometimes everyone needs to be. I'm saying we all were part of a pathway or series of pathways that called for rectifying. The future of ELP was at stake, there were enormous financial risks considered and contemplated that even for a band of ELP's stature would or could have resulted in a fatal blow and possibly receivership. None of us can say at this time what it all was about; we respect each other too much. But we now have a shared vision again and the fruits of our labor will be realized sooner than later, and for many years to come. We are committed to the concept of ELP as a lifetime band with many songs, and I believe many albums, yet to come.

Carl. I'm not lying if I were to tell you that at the beginning of the year [editor – 1976] the very future of the band was at stake. It really started before Winter's Light was released, but it came to a focal point then. We had to have some incredibly deep, heavy, tense discussions. It really reminded me of what we went through before going into the studio for Tarkus, but it was even more serious, if

74

that's the right word, maybe not. I thought the band was on the verge of...it was at a crossroads. There were some demands and some borderline farfetched views. I won't and can't say the details, but we have pulled ourselves back from the precipice, we are still here.

Chapter Two

Fanfare, 1976

Emerson, Lake, and Palmer

The Alternate History

1975-2000

In March 1976 ELP enter the studio, and in July release a single album titled Fanfare. The title cut – fully named Fanfare for the Common Man – is a huge hit UK #2, while C'est La Vie is a minor hit US #91. The album features Keith debuting the mammoth and technologically ground-breaking Yamaha GX-1 synthesizer, used exclusively on the title cut and Carl's features Food For Your Soul and The Enemy God Dances With the Black Spirits. For August through November, ELP embark on a condensed – compared to their mammoth early '70's undertakings – tour of the US and include a brief visit to Japan as well as a UK-only European swing.

Fanfare

Track listing

Side 1

1. Fanfare for the Common Man

(Aaron Copland; arranged by Emerson)

2. Lend Your Love to Me Tonight

(Lake, Peter Sinfield)

3. Toccata Con Fuoco

(Emerson)

Side 2

1. The Enemy God Dances with the Black Spirits

(Sergei Prokofiev; arranged by Emerson and Palmer)

2. Allegro Giojoso

(Emerson)

3. C'est la Vie

(Lake, Peter Sinfield)

4. Food For Your Soul

(Palmer, Harry South)

5. Andante Molto Cantabile

(Emerson)

6. Nobody Loves You (Like I Do)

(Lake, Peter Sinfield)

Keith. We're thrilled to have yet another hit in the UK, albeit from an American composer, which might strike some as a bit odd as we often refer to our European roots musically. But, to me, Fanfare is this triumphant statement, a vision one could call it I suppose, about all the US soldiers that came to Europe during World War 2. Soldiers, common men, having their lives interrupted to fight for our freedom, not just theirs or for America. Perhaps that's the underlying reason why the perception of the song resonates with, shall we say, British national sentiment, or history. I'm not sure, but it is something to think about as we're 30 years on since the end of the war. I mean, would England have survived without America's assistance? After all, we were basically bankrupt, something about not paying back loans after World War 1, right? And surely Russia wouldn't have survived either? Did they pay back America? Oh dear, I'm going to get myself in trouble here. [Pretends to talk into a flower vase on the table] "Ivan, did you get that last? Boris, how about you?" Anyway, I'm sure there's no harm done since touring Russia isn't a remote possibility, probably not in my lifetime. Maybe someday I'll get to play Nutrocker in Moscow; wouldn't that be sublime.

Greg. Fanfare is an interesting paradox for ELP as we have somewhat blues'ed up an American classical piece. Usually it's the European classical pieces that get the ELP treatment, but we've done something with an American classical piece that could be in the vein of typical blues inspired rock, something we're not really known for, right? It's definitely not usually what we do. Fanfare is a stirring and timeless piece of music. For those that enjoy our version, I would encourage you to explore Copland's Third Symphony where the fanfare's main theme is also used; it's a wonderful piece of music. Keith's arrangement is just perfect; I knew he'd buy into it eventually.

Carl. Yes, yes, we've gotten many questions on what seems to be a fractured Side Two [sighs]. We had that with Tarkus as well if you can recall, also an infamous Side Two. I know a lot of fans are asking, "Is this the end of ELP and concepts, or concept albums?" Are we now going to follow the current trend or trends and become committed to short songs? Well, I can confidently say no, no...we haven't. Also, it's clear that Fanfare certainly isn't short, but it is an instrumental.

Carl. Certainly we're aware of popular trends and tendencies and such, we have been from the very beginning of ELP. Although, I think especially with Greg

78

coming into his own as a writer we might continue to see more than just one Greg song or ballad per album. At first we wanted to make sure we had a band album, but as we've established our identity, Greg's songs have consistently bridged that accessibility gap and now we've expanded upon that with Fanfare for the Common Man. We're still remaining true to the nature of the band, a European musical mindset, guiding us using rock music presentation styles. I don't think shorter songs throw the album off kilter. I mean, if they were terrible songs there might be a worry, but they're not.

Keith. I imagine it's easy to look at the tracks and the credits and go, ah, he really didn't write anything substantial for this record, did he? But I assure you, rearranging a piece to make it work isn't a walk in the park. There are so many things to consider, you know? I mean, firstly, you have to do justice to the piece, and then you have to make it work in a band setting and get the others to buy in on the vision. And, it's true, sometimes it does work easier with some pieces than others. With Fanfare for the Common Man did it come about easier than others? Yes, it did. But, I've experienced other times when original compositions just flowed and it was much easier than an adaptation. Abaddon's Bolero is an example of that.

Greg. Working with Pete, my acoustic songs definitely have taken more of a consistent romantic slant. C'est la Vie of course is a bit melancholy compared to Lend Your Love to Me Tonight and Nobody Love You Like I Do, but they all have this basis of romantic yearning. Compared to ELP's suites, the subject matter is a bit different, but really, the themes of love and loneliness have been a foundation of rock and literally all types of music from the very beginning.

Carl. So many bands run out of steam after their first album, that's what you practice and write for, possibly for years, right? Then, there comes the challenge of the dreaded follow-up. When I see what we've come up with for Fanfare, considering the run that we were on and that smallest of breaks for Winter's Light, we really have maintained an outstanding level of quality, for the collaborative pieces but also what Keith and Greg brought forward and now with my contributions as well.

Keith. Yes, there is the new electronic addition to my arsenal that's not Moog or Hammond. This album has given me the opportunity to debut the stunning new Yamaha GX-1 synthesizer. Don't ask me how much it cost; I still startle myself when I look at the receipt. Thanks to the success of Father Christmas I think I at least got back my investment [laughs], but that's about it! At first I was completely mesmerized by it, and I still am; it is an incredible machine, truly. But Greg and Carl kept me on track, not to lose sight of the Hammond, the Moog, which I've come to accept as the signature keyboard sound of ELP, along with the piano of course and, I should add, Greg's voice and the acoustic guitar. I see the GX-1, and the many synthesizers that will follow in its footsteps, as an additional arrow in the quiver. I'm being told by Yamaha that the GX-1 is so ground-breaking that it will bridge the gap to the next generations of synthesizers, making them significantly more affordable and, I'm happy to report, portable. This is great news, but it comes a bit too late for my checkbook and the road crew's backs. I've painfully discovered over the years that you might be remembered for being the first in line, but it's never cheaper.

Keith. After I had the first preview of the GX-1, I had this thought that keyboards are the great unrespected instrument in rock. I mean, early on the piano had prominence with Jerry Lee Lewis or Little Richard, but the organ always seemed to be a bit cheesy and wheezy, you know, kind of parlor'ish and a bit wheezy. It's seen as a piece of furniture, something your grandmum kept as the decades went on. The GX-1 is a tremendous leap forward, but is it a landmark instrument that will change the attitude of guitar-centric rock fans or help bring synthesizers to the forefront in popular music? I'm not sure. Of course, there's also the matter that we don't play what you could call standard rock, so I don't know, but it could bring in fans of other styles that are intrigued by it.

Greg. All I can say about Side Two, in addition to all of them being quality songs, is that they are reflective of ELP at its most basic elements. You have Keith the pianist and composer, Carl as percussionist expanding his skill and arranger's palette, and myself as a singer-songwriter with a focus on the acoustic guitar. Was it consciously done? [Pause] Let's just say it came about naturally when our competing visions finally intersected and became complimentary, not necessarily without a strong discussion or two, which is ELP. But, I believe, we all believe, that the individual and collective works speak for themselves. Was it necessary? Absolutely and without question, yes, and timely as well.

Carl. Honestly, Fanfare was the easiest song ELP has ever recorded; it was just sheer, instant inspiration. When we looked back at all the hours and hours working on bits and pieces of Tarkus, Karn Evil, and the endless but necessary discussions, this was an absolute thrill. Keith is just starting to scratch the surface of the GX-1; it sounds a bit like a spacecraft, doesn't it? I predict he will have something amazing for the next album.

Keith. Yes, my two solo piano pieces are just that, solo piano...not my first choice however. My other ideas or suggestions were not completely acted upon...yet...so I asked they be on the album. I was told there was a mix-up in the final track listing and they were separated...it is unfortunate, a bit of a disappointment.

Greg. Following Father Christmas, Pete and I seemed to get on a roll and we put together a string of very nice songs, very heartfelt I think. I'm sure confidence in the wake of success plays some part of it. But even going back to our shared days in King Crimson, we already had worked well together there before mass acceptance. We may not have written directly together as he did at the time with Robert [Editor – Robert Fripp, King Crimson guitarist] and of course Ian [Editor – Ian McDonald, King Crimson multi-instrumentalist], but obviously there was a sympathetic element, a ready cooperation, which led to our current situation.

Carl. The Prokofiev piece [editor – The Enemy God Dances With the Black Spirits] is so well suited for percussive accompaniment, especially with my style and understanding of orchestral percussion. I have to give a lot of accolades to Keith for agreeing to work on the piece and to digest all the parts; it's quite daunting with the multiple counter melody lines. It's a wonder how he keeps it all straight and manages to pull it off.

81

Keith. Reflecting, I was surprised to see the orchestral and emotional connection between Janacek's [editor – Leos Janacek, Czech composer] Sinfonietta [editor – his orchestral work from 1926], which formed the foundation for Knife Edge, and Fanfare for the Common Man. Sinfonietta was dedicated to the Czech Army, an exhortation to victory I suppose, and of course Fanfare for the Common Man has that same motivation, a rallying cry for the people. Both pieces have that trademark heavy brass and stately percussion as well, which simply adds to the martial splendor.

Greg. This is a unique album for ELP, with two hits, you know. Obviously we've had some singles success on both sides of the Atlantic, but with two different songs and having one on the charts on either side, I think it's a unique achievement for us. I should add of course, I'm sure it's been done many times by bands like the Beatles or Rolling Stones, but for ELP or any progressive band, it's a very nice thing. It's also interesting to note that they are two different, very different songs stylistically, but still uniquely ELP featuring our trademark sound or sounds.

Carl. This album developed very unusually, all three of us had an informal collection of tracks to bring in, and then that's how they were recorded. It reminded me of the debut, very individually focused and oriented with a few obvious collaborations. For me personally, the big difference was that I was able to bring something in as a composer, not necessarily just as a drummer, as with Tank. As we've learned, and are learning, over time ELP works in many different ways.

Keith. I've been asked if Fanfare for the Common Man was something too obvious that The Nice would have done, with their history of classical adaptations. Well, this certainly isn't the first classical adaptation ELP has done, but no, I don't quite think so...well, maybe. Sometimes an idea takes forever to form beyond a theme or the others might not have the same vision of that introductory idea, if anything that would have been Pictures at an Exhibition. In other circumstances, an idea can catch fire immediately with everybody, everybody understands the direction you're going and it's on. That is essentially what happened with Fanfare, it was near instant understanding and development. By taking this stripped down approach, it certainly simplified the structure and arrangement and allowed us to work with the improvisational part as we saw fit.

Greg. I see Keith's arrangement of Fanfare for the Common Man as uniquely ELP, despite knowing Keith's history with The Nice. Firstly, ELP is a lot more precise in its playing and Keith's use of space on Fanfare is something which I never heard with The Nice so much, let alone the uniqueness of the GX-1.

Carl. I'm finding tremendous satisfaction in adapting classical pieces, so I certainly understand where Keith is coming from. While Keith obviously has a fuller harmonic understanding of the music, it's just as hard work for me as I have an obviously bigger challenge in finding something that has an inclination towards a percussive element, or is perhaps more rhythmically oriented such as The Enemy God.

Chapter Three

Pirates, 1977

Emerson, Lake, and Palmer

The Alternate History

1975-2000

ELP return to the studio in June 1977 and in September release a single album titled Pirates. The album's epic title track once again features Keith on the Yamaha GX-1 for which they also enlist the help of a full orchestra for the first time since recording I Believe in Father Christmas. Keith's interpretation of Honky Tonk Train Blues is a hit in their home land as it hits UK #21, but does even better in Italy hitting IT #1 and becoming the theme song to the popular Italian TV show Odeon. Starting in October 1977, the band undertakes its first large-scale tour of the USA since 1973. Surprisingly little is played from Winter's Light, but there is a reasonable emphasis on Fanfare; the setlist is then completed with truncated versions of their previous epic pieces. In order to present Pirates the way it was recorded, ELP only play it in specific cities where a local or regional symphony orchestra can perform in support of the piece. This unusual approach, naturally, created huge anticipation at dates that were primarily in the larger coastal cities and some world cities, such as Chicago; it also created some disappointment with the fan base outside of those areas.

As the tour worked its way into early December, the orchestra was then also added to I Believe in Father Christmas as the show finale. At shows where there is no orchestra, the band plays a full version of Tarkus and Keith personally commits to playing an extended piano improvisation. The full version of Tarkus and the piano improvisations, in turn, are not played at any of the orchestral dates. Watching Over You is also released as a single, but does not chart. In the wake of a new epic piece with Pirates, fans ask, is the progressive, conceptual side of ELP back?

Pirates

Track listing

Side 1

1. Pirates

(Emerson, Lake, Peter Sinfield)

2. Hallowed Be Thy Name

(Lake, Peter Sinfield)

Side 2

1. Watching Over You

(Lake, Peter Sinfield)

2. Honky Tonk Train Blues

(Meade Lux Lewis; arranged by Emerson)

3. LA 77

(Palmer)

4. Closer to Believing

(Lake, Peter Sinfield)

5. Marche Militaire

(Franz Schubert; arranged by Emerson and Palmer)

Keith. [Deep breath] Is ELP back? I don't think we ever truly left, did we? I hope not. I know a few of our die-hard fans were not overly pleased with the last two albums, and I know this will probably raise some eyebrows, but I wasn't either...not completely anyway. Not that the success wasn't welcomed, but I never thought of ELP as a singles-oriented band. That's the era where we come from; releasing singles or consciously writing a single? That never motivated us; no singles, ever. I know Lucky Man and From the Beginning gave us AM radio profile early on and we were fortunate to have many of our album cuts played on FM with AOR format. But it was the futuristic pieces like Tarkus, Endless Enigma, and Karn Evil 9 that started to cement our overall legacy and how music history will see us having an impact on the rock genre. I firmly believe Pirates will also attain the same status in the ELP canon of epic tunes.

Keith. The truth is, I compromised in 1975, or maybe the word is bargained, but I wasn't happy. And while I can't divulge all that was done or not done...in the end, it helped the band, I believe it saved the band. It might not have helped me and elevated my profile as a composer then and there, but by virtue of the band having weathered that tumult, I am now in a place where the continued success and presence of ELP truly allows me to focus as a composer, a composer of pieces whose life will go on beyond ELP.

Greg. We wanted to be judicious in working with the orchestra; this is still ELP, not ELP unable to present its music without an orchestra. From the band's beginning we've focused on being able to present our studio material in a live setting, with the energy and excitement that comes with live performance. We did lose the script a bit with a few songs on Trilogy and the overabundance of overdubs. After all, it was technology progressing and we were getting caught up in maximizing the possibilities. But, I believe we made up for it with the quality of the material on that record and of course on our subsequent releases where we focused on being able to play the material live.

Carl. I hope the other two are ready for me to use an orchestra; it's my turn to hold the ball, first there was Greg, then Keith! I have some very interesting ideas. I mean, I'm not one of the main writers in the band right now, but having seen Greg and now Keith harness the power of an orchestra in how they present their compositions, I feel like I now have the confidence as a percussionist and a composer to explore this. This is not something for beginners; I couldn't have done this shortly after ELP formed.

Keith. You've heard the story of the movie score, right? So, I had wanted an orchestra, even going back to The Nice as the thought and concept of an orchestra is very inspiring, very fulfilling. For Pirates, the music and the lyrics demanded this grand treatment. We could do it as a three-piece as a 3-piece and the volume in a live concert setting should offset the absence and impact of an orchestra, especially thanks to the GX-1. But to have that orchestral wall of sound, it's just, it's beyond glorious. I was very much anticipating using the orchestra on Con Fuoco, it should have been...well, it works so well. I hope someday to perform the other two piano pieces from the Fanfare album in conjunction with this latest one, ideally with an orchestra, but don't tell Greg and Carl [laughs]. Having Greg and Carl play on the Con Fuoco piece was something I had not visualized, not immediately. But when I played it in rehearsal they joined in and it just took off. Because it is a dramatic and aggressive piece, it works very well in a rock context. It is the unexpected beauty of working in a band setting, I guess I just didn't see it that way at first, which has happened before and will probably happen again.

Greg. We had experience with an orchestra with [I Believe in] Father Christmas. Keith of course, had that experience with The Nice, and Carl is very well-versed with orchestral percussion technique. Keith is very enamored with the orchestra, it's just the matter of us finding the select piece or pieces that it works well on. We, ELP, are too dynamic of a band to be stifled by an orchestra, live that is. Well, I don't mean that in a bad way, because the orchestral musicians tend to be very good, very disciplined, but in rock you don't necessarily always need that overly strict discipline.

Carl. The orchestra...an orchestra...yes, maybe ELP should just get its own orchestra, the EL Philharmonic! I must say that Greg did great production work on my piece Food For Your Soul, he really encouraged Keith to arrange the horn parts from Harry South to make it a bit more ELP-like.

Keith. Well, it's both a blessing and a curse to have an ever-expanding catalog to choose from. I do miss playing Karn Evil in its entirety, and especially with Pictures [editor – Pictures at an Exhibition] the ebb and flow leading up to the Great Gates [editor – The Great Gates of Kiev] is, in my opinion, sorely lacking, as is Tarkus by missing certain sections, but...what do you do, what can you do? We've already had to chop some of these pieces up. We can't play four hours every night, so we try and present the latest of what ELP has come up with and also a healthy regard for the past. Like with any other band that has an expanding catalog, live set lists are living, breathing things that reflect that current mindset of the band and its fans. Who knows what material will be part of an ELP live set in the future?

Greg. It's not so much a matter of priorities, but presenting ELP live as a band that continues to progress, it's not easy. We have an unusual dilemma where we have so many lengthy compositions that are loved by the fans. So many of our fans show up with all the records, they know all the tracks, all of them, you know? We want to support the new record and expose people to it in a live setting, but we don't want people to feel they've been short-changed when they want to hear all of Karn Evil or when sections of Pictures are left out...I miss it as well. Sadly, in that regard we cannot please all of the fans all of the time; I do take it very seriously, as does the rest of the band.

Carl. Well, thankfully we came to an agreement that we didn't want the attention on ELP being consumed by the possibility of failure...I'm sorry what was the question again? [Laughs] It feels like we are moving forward in the spirit of, say around 1972. We have a new, epic track to share which is being presented in a very unique way. It feels that we are deliberately assuming the progressive
88

mantle again which, in this day and age, is like wearing a 'Kick Me' sign, which we continue to do quite proudly.

Keith. Right, well, thankfully Stewart [editor – Stewart Young, ELP manager] is a master organizer and negotiator. Working with the orchestra in any capacity is a dream realized. You should hear what I hear in my head when we play Knife Edge or Pictures [at an Exhibition] and imagine the orchestral embellishments; it would be amazing. While at first I had my own opinions regarding ELP using an orchestra, I now see the value of using it sparingly, much like the GX-1, to not dilute the ELP sound...or the ELP checkbook! [Laughs] I hope that our fans understand this is not a carrot and stick situation, and I do feel a sense of contrition that we cannot perform Pirates with an orchestra to our fan base in the central or southeastern parts of the United States. I hope one day to present our complete live performance in an orchestral fashion. I believe the future of synthesizers could very well be the tool to make this happen, from a purely sonic perspective.

Greg. I have to give credit to Keith regarding the idea of using an orchestra, and I know he credits Carl and me with the vision as to how best to employ it within the greater scope of the band. There is no doubt that when the orchestra kicks in on Pirates it is absolutely hair-raising, and for the final crashing notes of Father Christmas, as unbelievable as it was in the studio, it is astounding live.

Carl. Keith and Greg have no idea what I have in store for them! [Laughs] I have been formulating some amazing orchestral ideas from a compositional perspective. But, anyway, yes using the orchestra, so... One can't complain about the sonic aspect, but I do find that I have to get in a different mindset for Pirates. It's no longer three people locking in musically, but you're pulling along an additional 40, 50, or so people where we're hopefully all on the same page with only minimal full rehearsal. Don't get me wrong, these are wonderful, talented musicians, but they obviously work in the classical realm and the push-pull of a live, rock context might be a bit unfamiliar to them. For Father Christmas I actually have it easy, just two big hits and it's thank you, good night!

Keith. God bless Stewart, he knows the band, and I really feel like he knows me. He did Herculean work arranging the various orchestras to support ELP on the select dates for Pirates. He actually showed me the numerous charts and schedules with all the moving parts; I can only guess how times he burned the midnight oil while literally living on North End Road [editor – office location of ELP's own label Manticore Records in Fulham, London]. It looks like he was designing an atomic bomb! I mean, he has the patience of a saint to deal with this, all of this; he is a wizard.

Greg. Just as the band worked to make my acoustic pieces work within the band context, I really wanted to help Keith realize the use of the orchestra as it's very important to him personally and as a composer. Because of that, it's important to me. I must admit that while I had my reservations with the orchestra at practically all levels, but when everything is firing on all cylinders, and that includes performing with the orchestra, I believe we are unbeatable.

Carl. As someone with a classical upbringing and background, the orchestral approach and application of symphonic percussion comes very natural to me. We were considering various options on how to incorporate the orchestra, not musically, but logistically and administratively; mind you, it's not an easy thing, as there are massive points to ponder. I do believe the approach we're taking is the near perfect balance between an artistic vision and a good business approach.

Keith. We're often asked if ELP lost its sense of humor after Brain Salad Surgery. I'm sure this refers to songs like The Sheriff or Jeremy Bender, and of course Benny the Bouncer. Well, Benny is actually quite dark, dark humor I suppose. But, I do see their point, as the first album had the acoustic guitar interlude on Take a Pebble which was rather jovial, if that's the right word. Yes, I can see that, sure...with Nutrocker and Are You Ready Eddy? as well, it seems we did make it an unconscious habit. I mean, while not outright light or humorous, I do think that the ragtime piano pieces have a certain levity to them, similar to Nutrocker I suppose. We do think about that, what could be a joke today could possibly cause some offense tomorrow, tastes do change over time. I think it's important that humor is not about being cruel; we wouldn't do that, but maybe making people laugh at something humorous or their own discomfort.

Greg. What made Pirates so enjoyable to work on lyrically was consciously shifting the natural progression ELP has made since the first albums where the lyrics have a strong, and I believe successful, emphasis of storytelling on a mystical or supernatural level, to a more conventional narrative, more grounded. Unconventional lyrics are effective in how they reflect upon or are reflective of the music; Jon Anderson of Yes understands this too. This is something critics never understood in regards to progressive music where the lyrics were dismissed as nonsensical rather than refusing to understand that meaningless in conventional terms does not mean lacking in subtle or vivid imagery.

Carl. We can tell that radio has changed, especially in America. The days of Pictures [editor – ELP live album Pictures at an Exhibition] being played in its entirety are gone, unfortunately. And while we have quite a number of songs that are more traditional in length and form, our signature pieces are the longer ones. We are lucky in that Greg has written a number of radio-friendly tunes, this in turn exposes our more progressive material to a wider audience should they want to investigate the band. I'm sure this has helped our level of exposure; it is unique how different elements drive people to check out ELP.

Keith. I've been asked by some people if I, or ELP, are losing our European connection somewhat. We recorded Fanfare [editor – Fanfare for the Common Man], an American composer's work [editor – Aaron Copland] and then there are some observations that Pirates has a tinge of Americana to it as well, beyond just the obvious connection with old Hollywood. I mean, compositionally there are some Tarkus like moments, lots of fourths, open fourths, but it certainly doesn't have the harshness of Tarkus, perhaps that is due to the orchestra and it is more of a single, flowing piece. But both Fanfare and Pirates, their main themes, are obviously European in nature, despite the obvious American origins or influences.

Keith. While Manticore Records was ultimately a Greg idea along with Stewart [editor – Stewart Young, ELP manager], I think many of our critics missed what we were trying to do. It wasn't just about solely promoting or servicing ELP. I mean, we were the label's premier act of course, so we are going to receive a certain amount of attention, and we benefitted. But it really was an honest to goodness label with talent being sought out on both sides of the Atlantic.

Greg. When one mentions Manticore Records, the first reaction is always that of course it was exclusively designed to advance ELP's career; of course it was an obviously ELP egomaniac venture. That wasn't the case at all, not at all. While ELP was the cornerstone artist of Manticore, I believe we did diversify quite heavily with our acts and we really did consciously seek out genuine talents. I don't mean the obvious ones like Pete Sinfield or acts like PFM and Banco [editor – Italian progressive rock bands] which were known to be affiliated with ELP and are progressive in style and nature, but we had some great heavy rock with Stray Dog [editor – American hard rock band] with the fantastic Snuffy Walden on guitar. We also managed to land a really great singer-songwriter with Keith Christmas [editor – UK] who had a Bowie connection. Then we had some genuine balladry and funk rock with a band called Thee Image [editor – US]. I mean, you can't get more un-ELP than those examples I would think. Most surprisingly, we also had the legendary Little Richard who released the great song Call My Name on the Manticore label.

Carl. Manticore Records was a wonderful experience to discover, mentor, and guide some of these genuinely talented people both as it relates to the music business and music itself. We hoped to share our own professional experience and knowledge, to give some of these artists a chance, a roadmap, or at least a good introduction to the business. It really was a different era then, even though it wasn't so terribly long ago. But, by 1976 we figured we'd had a good run and we were very busy with ELP as we were moving from a well-known act to being a truly established band. We had a contact stateside who knew that Motown was looking to expand into the rock market, so they took over distribution, but we decided to pull the plug on it now [editor – 1977] once we knew things were settled. Interestingly, I just heard that Moody Blues' own label [editor – Threshold] also folded.

92

Chapter Four

Memoirs, 1978

Emerson, Lake, and Palmer

The Alternate History

1975-2000

Following the conclusion of the tour supporting Pirates in February 1978, ELP enter the studio in June and release a single album, Memoirs, in August. As an album that can only be described as true to the progressive genre, Memoirs contains two full-length pieces each taking up an entire side (excepting one short song on Side One). Interestingly enough, Keith worked on the Memoirs piece by himself with Peter Sinfield, and Carl worked on his Concerto with Joseph Horovitz. Greg contributed production and just one co-composition to the album – The Gambler, the one short track on the album – which is released as a single, but does not chart. ELP goes on tour in September, and the band initially plays a shortened version of Memoirs; they had already stated in pre-tour interviews that Carl's percussion concerto would not be a possibility for live performance, not even partially. Very shortly into the tour, Memoirs is dropped and replaced by a full-length version of Tarkus. Greg also performs a very short and slow unidentified acoustic piece which he introduces as, "This one didn't make the cut." He, nor Keith and Carl, ever identifies the song. The fans start referring to it as Times and Crimes of Yesterday, from a line in the song that seems to stick out. At the mid-point of the tour, the band incorporates an arrangement of a big band number The Man With the Golden Arm [editor - from the 1955 movie of the same name] on recommendation of Carl as the vehicle for his drum solo.

Memoirs

Track listing

Side 1

1. Memoirs of an Officer and a Gentleman

a. Prologue/The Education of a Gentleman

(Emerson, Peter Sinfield)

b. Love at First Sight

(Emerson, Peter Sinfield)

c. Letters from the Front

(Emerson, Peter Sinfield)

d. Honourable Company (A March)

(Emerson)

2. The Gambler

(Emerson, Lake, Peter Sinfield)

Side 2

1. Carl Palmer: Concerto for Percussion

(Palmer, Joseph Horovitz)

Keith.   Yeah, so I hope this album kind of puts to rest the doubters who wonder if

ELP is still in the progressive camp. I mean, two extended pieces during this time of dance and disco, call it pop'ish if you'd like, vogue music. I'm very proud of Carl and his concerto, it's a wonderful piece. While Memoirs doesn't have the angry organ and sweeping Moog, it is a better paced composition, I think. I know that fans of our earlier work have an extreme affinity for that aggressive, rapidly evolving type of composition where you have jarring changes and shifts, time signature change here, key change there. I agree, it certainly is riveting and exciting when the music has unexpected departures. But, I believe that a piece like Memoirs as a part of our greater catalog develops ideas more, and in some ways better. I believe it has a certain element of maturity to it.

Keith. Yes, you heard it right, that definitely is a Chopin quote in Love at First Sight, and I believe it's from his Etude, Opus 10 [editor – Number 1, in C]. It's really a lovely, lovely bit and it just fit the mood of the track so well.

Greg. I've gotten many questions on this. The only thing I can say is look, I'm the band's singer, bass player, and guitar player, and of course I produce as well. It's not imperative that all my songs get on the record especially when there is quality music; my songs were always welcomed with open arms. Keith and Carl have been very kind to me over the years by allowing me to present what appear to be non-progressive songs and, just as importantly, making my songs work in the context of ELP. This is hard work for the band, not just for the writer. Besides, we all enjoy it when any ELP song does well, and I mean not just commercially. Groundbreaking artistry and technology is not always a guarantee for commercial success. But you know, Carl worked like mad, harder than I've ever seen him work on anything, and the results show it. He was worthy of any support we could provide; the commitment he displayed to his percussion concerto has injected the band with a renewed sense of loyalty and cohesion.

Carl. Remember my threats from a few years ago? Joseph Horovitz and I had been getting together, and this is the result. This is the pinnacle for me personally as far as compositional percussion, more than revolving drum sets, and more than synthesized percussion. Keith and Greg were totally supportive, I mean, how

95

many times does a drummer get a full album side completely to himself? Both Keith and Greg, in the meantime, are building up a surplus of tracks for our next album.

Keith. There was a push, a strong suggestion, from the record company that we explore going in a more commercial direction. Ahmet Ertegun [editor – co-founder and president of Atlantic Records] apparently had all sorts of plans for us to do...[mumbles]...commercial, radio friendly, you know, whatever. [Carl chimes in from the background, "I've got a good, new name for us, Keith and the Gang."] Right, absolutely, we have a very funny man there; thank you. But anyway, I think Ahmet and his brother, they own a football club somewhere, I think Chicago [editor – New York, Cosmos, American soccer team] and they had their hands full with something regarding some weighty business matters, so Stewart worked his magic and we managed to dodge that bullet. I heard later that Ahmet was at some romantic resort and was a bit unhappy when he heard that ELP had snookered him.

Greg. Peter and I always worked so well together, going back to King Crimson and of course with all the songs in between. But, he had some lyrics outside of Memoirs that just weren't ELP; I'm sure they'll work just fine for someone else. In the end, Keith helped us out on The Gambler, and that was it. It seems like a copy or derivative of Tiger in a Spotlight which is relatively simple, or simpler as it's basically a traditional three-chord rock song at heart. But it is a nice song in its own right, we wouldn't have included it on the record if it wasn't. After we had completed recording the album, Keith commented that it actually reminded him of some of the lighter-hearted tunes we had done before, like Jeremy Bender or The Sheriff. I might be able to salvage another song or two from the sessions Peter and I had, but it's not a priority right now.

Carl. This was not an easy album for me. You know, or you should know, this was many, many hours in the studio, recording, and writing, and recording, and re-writing...and let's not even talk about the rehearsals. I mean, it was a tremendous amount of effort. The other two know this, but I'm the only one who was on both sides of the album! Couple of bar stewards, those! [Laughs] Playing the concerto live is really not on the agenda for ELP, perhaps some time in the future when synthesizers become more powerful or when drums truly interact directly with synthesizers. I do hope, of course, that it is picked up in the future by orchestras to be performed.

Keith. I really don't know how or why I gravitated towards Peter's words. I think perhaps because the music I had at the time was more straight-forward, it wasn't quite as futuristic or other-worldly. And also, we're British, and we gravitate towards this prim and proper, stiff upper lip approach. But on the other hand, when the time comes, we also have an abundant reserve of a somewhat carefree, daredevil approach to life. You know, tally-ho squadron leader, Rule Britannia, that sort of thing where one looks at life and society through this prism of our history, the Union Jack, and you have these visualizations of exploring, maintaining the empire, you know? Peter's words just told this very, very British story, we all could relate to it, it's our history. I also felt badly for Peter who has been part of the ELP machine for quite some time, and then to see his writing relationship with Greg come to a halt; it was a bit sad. I felt compelled to use this substantial piece of work he had done, mostly because it was of significant quality. He worked quite hard at it, and I thought it suited the music very well; some of the parts were quite touching. On the other hand, the words for The Gambler were nice and light, that was just a fun story. The bridge has a kind of half-time, chic Caribbean flavor, which was accidental.

Greg. It was an odd thing with Peter, it used to work, but now it doesn't; I just don't know. And, I want it known that I or the others in the band certainly won't slag off on someone who contributed significantly to and will always be associated with numerous classic ELP songs. We wish Peter all and nothing but the best. We had an incredible run, the two of us. First starting with King Crimson, then committed to ELP, and of course I also helped him with guitar vocals and production on his solo album [editor – Still] which has some really wonderful parts. His words and mindset seem to resonate strongly with French or Spanish culture, perhaps that's where his work will end up.

Carl.   We owed the record company another album; this is true, really the same feeling, or the same situation, as in 1974-1975 where we wanted a break, a real break.   I know we had the Greatest Hits package ready to go last year, but something where we could legitimately let the ELP machine take a complete breather.   But, we were better prepared and had paced ourselves so that we had material ready, or at least I did! [Laughs] I think we were ready for it going back to 1977, which is what prompted Keith to get cracking, live and learn.

Keith.   We were a bit at odds with the record company over the cover art, which was rather unusual. I think they were a bit unsettled about the military theme of Memoirs, which, I'm not really sure why, because it has nothing to do with the stand-off in Europe between the West and East. Perhaps Viet Nam is still too fresh in people's minds, too hurtful, or maybe it's Afghanistan now. It's rather a puzzle especially since our tale is a historical one; it's not commentary or criticism of government of any sort.

Greg.   The record company really missed it in this case with the battle, excuse the term, we had over the cover of Memoirs. It's really quite unusual and unexpected considering how close we worked with them on and cooperated on all aspects of records we have made in the past.   The notion that Memoirs is some kind of political statement is rather absurd.   It's quite easy to see that this is a personal story, a rather sad one at that, of living through the war and the terrible consequences. I mean, it basically has an anti-war message, or at least that war is always dreadful at any level. There's nothing romantic about it, or about war. We English know very well that war is very palpable, very real, actually.   This is something all Europeans are actually quite aware of, sad to say.

Carl. I think that the art department didn't get, or read the whole story, if you will, and jumped to a rather childish conclusion. ELP's lyrics have had an anti-war slant to them, you know, songs like Lucky Man, Battlefield, this is nothing new or hidden. So, measure by measure, we set them straight and reassured them that we're not beating the war drums or some similar nonsense. The cover of the classic, stoic British officer at the front in the elements actually turned out quite well.

Keith.   Right, Memoirs...Memoirs, yes, well.   The struggles with Memoirs, it started in the tour rehearsals, pre-production, as I can best recall it. It had nothing to do with anyone not being on board giving less than 100%. But the piece starts out so, so subdued, and remains so for a while. I do still think it's quite nice. One of the few music writers on our side, I can't tell you who 'cos, um, I don't want to ruin his career [laughs], but he's incredibly fair, and cruel. I had invited him along to our tour rehearsals and he told me, "Keith, mate, this sounds great on the hi-fi with a glass of wine and a bint on the settee, but this won't work in concert with ELP, people want their teeth rattled". [Deep breath] Shockingly, for a writer he was right, quite right. We then modified the arrangement, much like we've done with our other extended pieces like Tarkus and Pictures for example, to grab the highlights, punch it up you know. But, it just was falling flat, no matter what we did. We had the arrangement pared down, and it was solid, but the live reaction, it was a bit of a shock for ELP.

Keith.   After the sixth, seventh, or eighth show, we all sensed, simultaneously it seems, that Memoirs, while appreciated by the fans judging by more than acceptable record sales, just didn't translate live compared to our other material, even if it is new for us and the audience. The reaction, the feedback, just wasn't there. We're mature enough now to recognize when a piece will eventually click. Our first forays with Karn Evil 9 were a mixed bag at first as well, but with Memoirs, it was very different, and very puzzling. With Greg's and Carl's encouragement and prodding I brought in more Hammond to the arrangement in an attempt to bring some energy into the music, some vitality, even the GX-1 a bit more. The Korgs are wonderful instruments, but they require a lot of finesse to bring them to the forefront both in the studio and live. It's difficult to compare Memoirs to the power of the Hammond and the Moog presented in the classic ELP material. I felt obliged to have at least something from the Memoirs suite in our current concert, so I arranged for a substantial section of The March [editor – the final section of Memoirs, Honorable Company (A March)], to interpolate with Aquatarkus, and that has actually worked out quite well, if I say so myself...while playing it all on the Moog!

Greg. Memoirs, at this time does not appear to be connecting with our audience, our long-standing fans, at least in a live setting from what we can determine. I don't think it has anything at all to do with the quality of the composition or its musicality. Memoirs – in my opinion – continues ELP's reputation for making fine records, but one never knows really until something is released. We liked it, one we could hope that our audience would as well. Perhaps it is a composition that is just out of time, perhaps it would have done better in 1973 or 1974? You know, I thought for sure Pirates was going to eclipse Tarkus and maybe even Karn Evil 9, and that didn't quite happen. But I do think Keith and Pete did a fine job with the piece; it deserves to be a recognized element in ELP's canon of long, multi-part pieces.

Carl. I did my best to give Memoirs some drammatico when it came to playing it live, you can look that up in your music theory book [laughs]. This has been the first time we've experienced something like this. There's always the danger of being over-confident; not that we were, or were automatically assuming a new piece's acceptance. It was all very ELP-like as the music was presented, we argued a bit as we should, and then we got on with it. During pre-production I had a bit of an inkling that it might be too soft for ELP, especially live, but [ruefully] my excuse is that I was knee deep in my concerto.

Keith. One has a tendency to second guess, and then doubt creeps in, either personally or for the direction you voted for, it can be fatal for an artist, or a band. I remember Greg being worried when the initial reactions to Karn Evil were a bit muted before Brain Salad Surgery's release, but we carried on and it worked out great. With Memoirs, it just felt that way with all three of us, which is very unusual, and also very interesting. In a way, the very positive aspect from this somewhat negative experience has made us realize how more musically connected and intuitive we have become with each other.

Greg. I can't and don't blame Keith, or Pete, or Carl. We all put our collective backs into it and agreed to work on it, and to make it work. With Memoirs being dropped from our set, I felt that we were short-changing our audience by not giving them the new music. The reaction to the classic material continues to be and remains very positive, thankfully.

Carl. We reached a certain point where we all agreed, this is not a do or die situation with Memoirs. It may not have been what we hoped for, but it's not the end of it all, we can work through this, the ship's not taking water and we can move on.

Greg. So, I had this piece that Pete and I worked on during the Memoirs sessions. It wasn't very ELP-like and by the time it was worked up it was too, um, happy. You know, baby, I miss you, which is VERY un-ELP-like [laughs]. So, I kind of reinvented or reworked it to make it like the more melancholy or thoughtful songs, like C'est La Vie which I also wrote with Pete. [Greg is asked about the title] I don't have a title, and I don't feel it needs one; it's just something new I wanted to share with the fans for this tour, probably this tour only. [Editor – when told of the title fans have given it, Times and Crimes of Yesterday] Well, now, isn't that so very nice. It's very much better than what Pete and I had for a working title and no, I'm not going to tell you what it was! [Laughs] I certainly don't want to give the impression that Pete is persona non grata, I will always have very, very fond memories of us working together, and there always will be a connection. As a matter of fact, I just heard that In the Court of Crimson King [editor – King Crimson's debut album] finally went gold in Canada. So there you have it, even when you no longer work with people, if you've done something positive and substantial, it will come back to you in that manner, eventually.

Carl. With Memoirs being dropped and there being no reasonable way of presenting the percussion concerto live, well, we did briefly discuss the possibility of presenting it live the same way we did Pirates. But honestly, does anybody except for the true die-hard fans want to hear my percussion concerto and then my regular solo too? But, I also realize that Pirates is totally different, it's a properly structured song, composition actually, with immediate broad potential and appeal. The percussion concerto is just more specialized, more discerning I suppose.

Carl. But anyway, since the concerto is a no-go live, I wanted to do something new, that is, new for the fans and also drum-related. For some reason, to many in my generation from the UK, The Man With the Golden Arm is just a classic score by Bernstein [editor – Elmer Bernstein, American composer and conductor], and the wonderful performance of Shelly Manne [editor – Sheldon 'Shelly' Manne, American jazz drummer]. Keith and Greg liked it, Keith more so, I think. I ran into Steve Howe [editor – Yes guitarist] earlier this year and he heard our arrangement and mentioned how he's also always loved it, maybe it was something in the Griffin's biscuits. I don't see us recording it, it's something to make up for the Memoirs shortfall for this tour or that the percussion concerto won't have a live outing. Does that sound bad? [Laughs] It's also an opportunity to do my solo within another tune. And of course, Keith does a wonderful arrangement with the synths and the reaction has been, thus far, very encouraging.

Keith. I remember while recording Memoirs, which was very enjoyable actually, either Greg or Carl mentioned during the many playbacks that the piece struck them as very serene, but not in a negative way. We have other pieces that have elements of serenity, Take a Pebble, Trilogy, Greg's acoustic numbers. I keyed in on that later, so while listening to the final version and when Letters [editor – Letters from the Front] started I had this inkling that perhaps this piece is missing the outrage or grandiosity of our other longer pieces, or at least the more drastic peaks. But, I mean, I do believe it is a fine piece as it is. But do we want to be known as the band with the obvious follow-up material, you know, Karn Evil 10, Endless Enigma Part 4? I don't believe our fans want or expect that.

Greg. There is something regarding Memoirs in a live setting that made us take notice, that it's almost as if there has been some kind of cultural change with live concert settings. Take a Pebble starts out very quietly also and yet, there seemed to be instant acceptance when the band started and even when we play it now. Maybe attention spans have gotten shorter? Our audiences tend to be more cosmopolitan, and always have been, so this is kind of a mystery.

Carl. We're not worried, honestly. With our track record, which I believe to be quite exceptional, to have a bit of a bump is not a reason to panic or abandon ship. I mean, most artists would be thrilled to have had a very, very solid 10 years like we've had. This isn't like we've undermined ourselves; we'll continue to broaden our knowledge as to what makes ELP work and not work.

Keith. We did discuss that with the relatively soft reaction to Memoirs in a live setting if we're witnessing the natural arc of our music and that we're perhaps on a downward trend now. Should we have continued along the dark and aggressive path that we established with the debut and Tarkus? It was an identifiable strength of ours, although I will say that Trilogy, to me, was a very bright and positive record, but then Brain Salad Surgery was quite dark thanks to Karn Evil 9. Was this inevitable even earlier and we managed to sustain ourselves? I've spoken with some musicians whose bands deal with very heavy themes, not necessarily depressing, but dark, and they often say it would be nice to lighten up a bit, you know?

Greg. Popular trends are not hidden, we certainly are aware of them in the context of what we are presenting or planning musically. We did discuss the possibility that we had attained a certain highpoint or several highpoints if you look at 1973 or maybe 1975, and that a decline would be inevitable but hopefully manageable. How we would deal with that would have to be a very straightforward discussion at the time, it's pointless to try to predict. Also, trends can change so quickly; hip today, outmoded tomorrow. We simply do what we do.

Carl. One has to be honest when you experience a bit of a downturn, not necessarily a rejection, otherwise you're simply ignoring the obvious. I did consider that perhaps we were seeing a shift in the lifecycle of our music, with the level of popularity it had, that now it was our turn to feel the pain as other styles come to the forefront. But really, ELP were risk takers to a degree from the very beginning; are today's risk takers just as audacious as we were back in the day, at least musically?

Chapter Five

Triton's Seahorse, 1979-1980

Emerson, Lake, and Palmer

The Alternate History

1975-2000

The band comes off the road in January 1979, and takes most of the year off. As the year winds down, plans are formulated for ELP's upcoming 10-year anniversary in 1980. The band chooses to mark the occasion with consistent, but carefully limited and managed touring in the US and Europe starting in April, 1980. The setlist's emphasis is on the band's hits and a rotation through their epic pieces. The record company marks the occasion with an expansive greatest hits package including a VHS release of their music videos with some live archival footage entitled Karn Evil Gold. Half-way through the tour, the band does a limited number of incognito shows in smaller venues performing acoustically — piano, bass, acoustic guitar, and drums; no other instruments. With their intent to attract only the true, hardcore fans, the band advertises themself for these venues randomly as Triton's Seahorse, Ganton 9, Sirens of Titan, or Keith's Knickers.

At the tour's conclusion, Keith and Greg retire to their homes and write individually and collaboratively. Carl proves to be the exception, burning off energy doing interviews and actively searching for inspiration meeting other musicians and checking out other bands.

Carl. I simply can't believe it's been 10 years. It's been a mad dash, but when I see what we've done, even I'm a bit stunned and surprised. I guess I did make the right choice all those years ago. I know the critics will be more than sad that ELP is taking a year off, they'll have to find another target for their vitriol, although they need not worry, we'll be back soon enough.

Carl. I met this fantastic guitar player and songwriter named Johnny Nitzinger in Los Angeles while doing business with the folks from Paiste. Funny story, he's a bit of a character, so when I told him I wanted to meet at 1PM he thought I'd said 11PM. I said, "Johnny, why on earth would I want to meet someone regarding a business or professional matter at 11PM?" [Laughs] While leaving ELP was never even considered, I thought he was a talented guy and he took the opportunity to share some songs he wrote along with songs from a keyboard player named Todd Cochran, I believe. The ones that stick out [pause], let's see, one was called She's Dynamite, and I think the other track was called Air Age Children. If ELP circumstances were different, I might entertain the idea of trying a stab at this kind of pop-rock, but it would probably have to have a foundation or nod to some progressive element. I shared one of the songs with Greg and, let's just say he was kind, but not too impressed.

Carl. I had a surprise visit from Mike Oldfield while at home in Tenerife, he heard I was living there and he sought me out. He's an amazing composer as everyone rightfully knows with massive creative abilities; very, very prolific. As it was, we became friendly, and we talked about doing something when I got back to England, but ELP was just starting on the new record and there just wasn't any time. It's a shame, because I really would have loved to work with him, perhaps played on a track or two of his, explore a bit of collaboration. It's a funny thing about mentioning Mike, I was sitting at the coffee shop looking at Mount Teide and thinking of him just the other day. Just a very, very bright and lovely man.

Keith. Thankfully with the ELP catalog, we had a wealth of material that we could choose from to present acoustically. I found myself looking at all the albums, and it was almost an embarrassment of riches of material that we may not have played regularly or very much, and not just only my compositions. I mean, elements of The Three Fates, Infinite Space, even Tank on piano sounded very fresh.

Greg. While we haven't explored it yet, Keith adding purely piano to my pieces and me adding guitar to Keith's piano pieces opens up all sorts of sonic and arrangement possibilities. We just need to be careful that we don't overdo it as I think the fans still want to hear the songs as originally conceived, maybe not overly enhanced in any way. It certainly could work, it would require some attention.

Carl. Since ELP's music is so dramatic, we're focusing on emphasizing the purely harmonic drama rather than tremendous shifts in volume; it requires quite a bit of subtlety, especially with the drums. Of course, one doesn't want the drum arrangement to simply become all brushwork either. We're emphasizing a couple of obvious topics, presenting the music as initially written or conceived, and then displaying the core of the songs within these skeletal arrangements. In some ways it's actually more theatrical because the audience knows what's coming, and when they hear it in a new way, it creates some genuine excitement.

Keith. Whilst in my home studio, I sat back and found myself reflecting on keyboard technology and what I've seen in these past 10 or 15 years. From Hammond to Moog to the GX-1 and now to the state-of-the art Korg products, it's as if technology is ramping up so fast...too fast perhaps. I've always been up on technology and pride myself on keeping up with innovations...trends, whatever. But I truly foresee a time when the technology will become a concern...with complexity or specialization...or in my worst fears, an obstacle or maybe a crutch. Perhaps players and composers like me will have to realize that they can only be superficially familiar with what the technology can do, not the nuts and bolts of how it can be created like with the Moog modular. As a composer however, it's marvelous that limitless sounds as I conceive them can be brought to life instantly, my only concern is that the great flexibility I have with something like the Moog is potentially lost due to the creation of generic sounds by manufacturers and removing the individuality. Mere button pushing...artists using the same canned sounds over and over, it sounds rather dreadful, honestly.

Greg. There always will be a certain magic for me when it comes to the acoustic guitar. The ability to simply pick the instrument up and have instant sound every time is a wonderful thing. I know Keith feels the same way regarding the piano as does Carl with the standard kit, it is music at its purest which is one of the reasons, I believe, ELP's music resonates with certain people so much...not just musicians either. Since we are a three-piece, and our music is identifiable even when volume is reduced and electronic sounds are removed, it is our music's ability, in both melody and structure, to be perceived regardless of the means or sound levels.

Carl. There is something very gratifying when you strip down a song to its basic elements and when the melody presents itself, the arrangement and such, and it's instantly recognizable, and I do mean instantly. It is a hallmark of ELP and any other band with a catalog of great songs.

Keith. We have witnessed a change in our general concert-going audience, but this change is a great reward in that we can tell our audiences seem to be getting older with us. Yes, it's a bit of a shock, but also very charming. To think that someone has been coming to your concerts for over a decade, and maybe buying a record or two, you feel a sense of pride that it does resonate with people, over time.

Greg. I can't remember where we were, but we were in between numbers and some spiky-haired individual was bounding up down in front of us shouting, "Flared trousers, look, flared trousers!" Why he was there in the first place, I truly have no idea. He eventually was quickly and quietly led away by the event staff, who received just as much applause as we did.

Carl. I had a chat with an earnest young fellow with a clothes pin in his ear who came to see us play, and he made an interesting point. He said that electronic music was actually more punk, if that's still the right word, because the guitar was harder to play. I really had to think about that for a bit, because in a way he's right. If the objective is to make it so simple that it can be everyman's music, I imagine anybody could plug in a synthesizer and play a simple line or hold a note that has an exciting sound, or sound effect. Who would have foreseen that?

Keith. We discussed some options with the smaller, acoustic-oriented shows. We gave ourselves some options, you know, piano only, piano and Hammond, maybe a piano and a multi-function keyboard. At the end of the day, we went with the piano only; it's the most real representation of ELP. I mean, of course there are Greg's songs and the acoustic guitar, but for the lengthy and collaborative pieces, it always goes back to the piano.

Greg. It felt very natural presenting our material in this fashion; it shows the depth of the songs, the writing. I briefly considered using an acoustic bass, as we had some experience with a stand-up bass on Watching Over You, but I just wasn't happy with the sound; it sounded a bit sloppy. Thankfully we were able to find a great sound with the Alembic four-string to compliment the piano and drums. Obviously, it was a dream playing quite a bit of acoustic guitar for these shows.

Carl. We all went back to the basics, you know. I decided to use a kit substantially reduced in size to fit in with the show's motif, something close to my Noddy kit from back in the day. It would have been a bit comical showing up with my standard concert kit dwarfing everything else, not to mention that since we were emphasizing smaller venues to keep in line with the mysterious approach, I would have occupied half the stage. When playing on a reduced scale, the fine details of the arrangements become much more prominent and you simply can't run through them behind a wall of sound.

Keith. We actually had been kicking around the idea of Show Me the Way to Go Home since the Pirates record, the tour actually. A lot of people think it's an American show tune, but it's British through and through [editor – credited to the English songwriting team Reg Connelly and Jimmy Campbell]. We thought it would be a nice way to bring down the intensity of the big show. As it turned out, we never used it, but when this particular tour came up for discussion, we all knew this would fit.

Greg. Vocally, it [editor – Show Me the Way to Go Home] was a very enjoyable thing to do. I do regret a bit that being in ELP there are some vocal styles that I haven't had the opportunity to really explore such as country and western, maybe even gospel. ELP demands the ELP style, so this was quite nice being able to do so. Obviously it's been covered and featured more than a number of times. In England, many of us can remember our mums watching Coronation Street [editor – long-running British soap opera] and Show Me the Way to Go Home being sung by one of the characters in a memorable scene.

Carl. Show Me the Way to Go Home is such a versatile song; pop, show tune, sea shanty, whatever you'd like. And, while we could have smashed through it, it allowed ELP to briefly show some restraint in the form of a jazz combo, not hard-core jazz obviously and not quite as jazzy as the improvisations we did on the Brain Salad Surgery tour, but something different.

Keith. I don't think we'll ever set out to consciously do a fully acoustic album, although it could happen, and it would be very interesting. We've done primarily acoustic songs before or significant segments that are acoustic, but I don't know if an entire album would be too different from what ELP is known for? I'm not sure how it would be received or if it were to get a bit tiresome especially for those who love the Hammond or the aggression of our other pieces.

Keith. Even before the acoustic shows, I've been approached about doing more solo piano pieces outside of ELP, and maybe even some solo piano shows. To me, I think it would get a bit monotonous just seeing me playing the piano, but if there's an interest perhaps I can look into that. I think what is more likely is that I'll do a collection of piano pieces sometime in the future. I've actually added a couple of piano songs to the show, or arrangements, if you will. I've come up with what I think is an interesting take on the old English hymn, Good King Wenceslas. I'm sure there is some eye rolling going on, but when it comes to old hymns and Christmas, ELP has been there before right? Jerusalem and I Believe in Father Christmas figure quite prominently in the ELP catalog, so I'm not exactly going
110

totally off script. I also had an arrangement of Aaron Copland's Simple Gifts in honor of his 80th birthday, and to say that Copland has been a small but integral part of ELP's history is not saying enough. We've actually been getting more than a few strong suggestions to perhaps include Good King Wenceslas as a B-side on a future anniversary edition single for Father Christmas.

Greg. I thought Keith's arrangement of Good King Wenceslas was wonderful. Like Jerusalem, it's thoroughly recognized as British, but it's not as British or old as some would think. The music is Scandinavian, and the good king was actually from Bohemia from what I've read. But, what it really means to me, is that there is a connection with I Believe in Father Christmas as it brings back memories of those of us who didn't have much when growing up, or those who don't have much now, and Christmas time was about sharing the spirit of the season, looking out for those less fortunate, and giving of one's time.

Carl. The power of a piece should be able to come through on a single instrument, so Keith chose very wisely with Good King Wenceslas. Greg and I instantly were taken to it, it's iconic and so well-known, but not cliché at all.

Chapter Six

Wind of Steel, 1981

Kings of the Road - 1982-1983

Emerson, Lake, and Palmer

The Alternate History

1975-2000

In November 1980 ELP convene in the studio, and in June 1981 release a single album entitled Wind of Steel. The cornerstone of the album is a lengthy composition entitled For Those Who Dare. The band announces plans for its longest and most extensive world tour to date, scheduling dates in Europe, North American, Japan, and Australia. They plan on being on the road starting in July through February 1982 interspersed with small breaks. After another break, ELP are then back on the road from August 1982 to January 1983. ELP announce that they do not intend to go back into the studio until this tour is completed. It Hurts and Canario are released as singles, but do not chart.

Wind of Steel

Track listing

Side 1

1. For Those Who Dare

(Emerson, Lake, Palmer)

Side 2

1. For You

(Lake, Peter Sinfield)

2. Torero Rana

(Palmer, Ron Aspery, Colin Hodgkinson)

3. It Hurts

(Lake)

4. Big Horn Breakdown

(Billy Taylor; arranged by Emerson)

5. Canario

(Joaquin Rodrigo; arranged by Emerson, Lake, Palmer)

Keith. I would be lying if I say that I didn't miss playing live or spending hours in the studio, but I also would be lying saying that I missed relaxing. I feel like I am ready for another 10 years of beating my head against the wall [laughs]! Well, I think upon reflection of ELP's first decade I, and I should say we, have learned so much. I'm still shocked that we sustained ourselves, but as the '70's came to an end I also realized how very lucky we've been...as individuals, and the band. We had an amazing run. This album came together very quickly, probably because of the time off; there's just something very refreshing about just having this artistic energy being released, sensing goodwill, and seeing the material come together.

Pressure can be good; it can create aggression and tension. As a younger musician, it is a great motivation to prove one's worth, to the band, to other bands, along with the birds of course [laughs]. But as one gets older, it becomes a musician's pressure to live up to what you realize one day that this is what you do. I write music, and I perform on stage, this is what I do.

Keith. I know some fans clamor for more of the fantasy lyrics and concepts like Tarkus or Karn Evil 9, and I love that too and I know Greg will have more of that in the future. But, I honestly think Greg's lyrics on For Those Who Dare are some of the best he's ever done, it's very relatable and it's current. Actually, it's still fresh in everybody's minds simply because of the horror of it all. It does have bits and elements of Pirates, but there is also an element of Memoirs, but updated for today, and maybe just a bit better...sorry about that Pete, I do still love Memoirs though, although I might be in the minority. I mean, going all the way back to Jerusalem, really, we just can't escape waving the Union Flag.

Greg. Well, it's the motto of the British SAS, right? Seeing those lads step into the line of fire with the embassy rescue, it was just awe-inspiring to me, and to many others I'm sure. I also thought that it was an unintentional follow-up to Memoirs, somewhat loosely, even though I didn't have anything to do with those lyrics. This was more suited for these uneasy times; times of turmoil, turmoil that we didn't think would ever reach our shores. This is lyrically more observational than personal.

Carl. I, for one, was a bit adamant that we tackle a concept piece, an extended piece. We didn't exactly have a complete crisis of confidence after Memoirs, but sometimes you just have to get back on the horse, you know. I felt we had to stand by the courage of our convictions as to what we do, what we're known for, and quite frankly, what we do well. I still feel that Memoirs was of high quality, but at the end of the day, the audience lets their feelings known and you have to accept it. For me, I enjoyed the writing and recording in that unlike Memoirs, or even Pirates, this was something we all consciously worked on very closely together.

Keith. Although we're 10 or 11 years on, it's gratifying to see elements or trends from our debut still resonate today. We have an extended piece, and then some pieces that reflect upon each of us individually. I mean, I have some piano, Greg has his ballad, and even Carl has one of his characteristic, jazzy tunes. It's so odd in that we have this ability to put out an album that is both unbalanced in the variety, but balanced for what it's known for, you know? There aren't many bands where all the members have this ability to project strongly as individuals, or should I say, equally strong.

Greg. For You is probably the last song that I wrote, or will write, with Pete, and for sure the last Lake-Sinfield song to grace an ELP album. For the writing sessions of Memoirs, Pete and I just did not connect as he was bringing some lyrics in that were somewhat removed from what ELP is known for. Was the well running dry? No, I don't think so; I think we both just realized the dog had its day. But having said that, For You turned out quite well, I think. I think even Pete would agree that it's not our greatest work, but a very nice song. I have a feeling a talent like Pete will find the outlet he's searching for regarding the more commercial lyrical elements he has that don't suit ELP too well.

Carl. Well, Torero Rana is my compositional contribution, I've kind of brainwashed myself being in Tenerife. I think the Anglicized name, if you want to see for yourself, would have just looked wrong for ELP [laughs]. The lads from Backdoor [editor – UK jazz band] are very talented; Keith and Greg had to do some work to get the parts down, which they did of course in their very ELP-like fashion. And, of course ELP has this knack for turning three or four minute songs into six or seven minute spectacles.

Carl. When I brought in the demo for Torero Rana, Greg was rather adamant that the more improvisational horn parts and special effects be addressed or handled by Keith so we don't stray too far from what ELP fans expect. Greg has a great understanding of what the band needs to do to maintain this sort of proper musical image, or decorum. I mean, from the very beginning the critics accused us of being stuffy, haughty, and made it well known they thought we were disappearing up our own backside. That wasn't the only reason we've had some lighter fare over the years, like The Sheriff or Jeremy Bender. But, is that different really than any other bands where their style or approach dictates their means of presentation? Taking our art, which is our music first and only, seriously is what we've done and what we do.

Keith. This tour has been a monster in its own way, but in a way it's been easier than our tours from the early '70's. We're a little bit older and wiser and we need naps now after a few jars [laughs]. But, thankfully our management has paced it so much better that we're not just sprinting a bloody marathon. There are built in breaks and multiple dates in the same city or surrounding areas, which allows us to work on new ideas during soundchecks and such. It's wonderful not to be run ragged for months on end.

Greg. As this tour is winding down, I have to look back to 1970-1973 and wonder how we kept our individual and collective sanity; the pace, it was unending. I mean, there were wonderful elements, and once-in-a-lifetime memories and experiences, but lesser men would've cracked and retired to the countryside...we almost did...we talked about it. I'm very gratified that we're into our second decade and that the ELP family is as strong as it's ever been. The bonds, our bonds, are getting more and more secure as we continue to have positive experiences.

Carl. This tour, while much more extensive of course, reminds me of the Winter's Light tour [mumbling, "...that album title again."]. Not necessarily in scope, because we are going out with a full retinue, but the friendlier pacing, a bit more consideration. It's nice knowing what city I'm waking up in for a change. Where am I, Miami? I won't be going outside unless I'm in a tank, I'm going back to sleep.

Keith. We were thrilled to be going back to Japan and not only playing more dates than we had in the past, but also having a bit more time to visit the extraordinary country it is. Everyone is so respectful, I feel badly when an after show meet has to come to an end as everyone still has questions, but they always remain eternally polite and grateful.

Greg. Visiting Australia was another highlight among highlights, even for a band like us that has been on numerous international tours. We knew that Fanfare for the Common Man did well in Australia back in the day [editor – AUS #5, 1976] as did the album [editor – Fanfare, AUS #6, 1976]. So it was wonderful to hear that Stewart [editor – Stewart Young, ELP manager] was able to secure several dates and a couple of days off for us. I imagine it shouldn't be a complete surprise that Fanfare would do well in Australia as it did in the UK, you know, for obvious reasons; but one should never automatically expect the success at any level or location.

Carl. I was very much looking forward to going to Japan and engage in the type of conversations with fans you just don't find anywhere else. Well, you do, but not at the rate you do in Japan. I think the others maybe were a bit worried that there would be a drop-off from that absolutely manic tour in 1972. I mean, of course it's not the same because it was all completely new back then. But I sensed that ELP had really, really resonated with the fans there, it wasn't just a passing fancy, a one off. There was something about the combination of musical styles we're known for and the precision, the accuracy that just resonated there.

Keith. Big Horn Breakdown has long been a favorite of mine, and that style seems to be one of the things I'm known for. I was interested to find out that Billy Taylor, the composer, also wrote material for Charlie Parker [editor – legendary US jazz saxophonist and composer]. I've quoted Parker in the past as part of my live improvisations, and I have a very interesting idea for an arrangement of his signature standard Au Privave that I hope to do one day. But anyway, Big Horn Breakdown is the kind of tune you play and you can't help but smile; it's certainly not an easy song to play accurately at the effective tempo required.

Greg. It Hurts started out as one of my acoustic songs in the style of C'est la Vie, somewhat melancholy, but more introspective, I think. Both Keith and Carl suggested making it more of mid-tempo type ballad, a whole band song, and it worked out quite well. It gave Keith the opportunity to do one of his trademark,

117

extended solos. It's a shame it wasn't a bit more popular, but that's how these things go.

Carl. Canario is a wonderful piece that we've been kicking around since the Memoirs recording sessions. It's assumed to be quite an old piece, but it goes back only to 1953 or 1954 as part of the Fantasía para Un Gentilhombre suite, courtesy of the great Joaquin Rodrigo who is still with us. Many people aren't aware that Rodrigo lost his sight while still a young child and wrote his compositions in Braille, which is unbelievable really.

Chapter Seven

Yesterday's Hero, 1984

Keith at the Movies

Emerson, Lake, and Palmer

The Alternate History

1975-2000

Following the end of the 1981-1983 ELP world tour, which included the most comprehensive tour of Japan yet, the band reconvened in the studio in October 1983 and begin working on a new studio album. The more relaxed itinerary of the tour allowed for much jamming and sharing of material, and thus the band had a surfeit of material and was expected to be very prepared to deliver a classic ELP album. Or were they? In May 1984, the band release a single album, Yesterday's Hero. Upon the album's delivery, the music was totally not as expected based on the reports of intensive band rehearsals during soundchecks that were heavy on Keith presenting what observers described as cinematic music: short and intense bursts of interludes that vary from calming to unsettling without any type of obvious hints towards traditional or conventional song structures. The album contains no lengthy, progressive piece; instead it's heavy on mid-tempo songs written by Greg interspersed with a few Keith instrumentals and a live version of Peter Gunn recorded during the Fanfare tour. Even the most loyal ELP fans are somewhat mystified.

As was eventually learned, Keith was approached by the legendary Italian horror film director Lucio Fulci when ELP was in Rome regarding soundtrack work for one of his movies with the working title Kills With a Dance Step. Keith poured much of his new music into Fulci's movie which received the eventual title of Murderrock. The end result for ELP was their worst-selling and worst charting album to date, filled with MOR content loathed by the progressive community. When press talk immediately turned to questions of the band breaking up as a result of Keith's absence or the decoys placed, Greg and Carl were surprisingly at ease with the situation, even hinting that they were aware and supportive of Keith's intent and actions. Following the release of Yesterday's Hero, the band announces there will be no plans to tour in support of the album. Keith remains out of the public eye with the exception of one interview where he discusses the motivation for what seems to be a sabbatical from ELP. I Don't Know Why and Haunted are released as singles but do not chart. However, I Believe in Father Christmas briefly re-enters the charts, peaking at UK #84 at Christmas time, giving the seemingly beleaguered ELP camp something to cheer about before the year's end. Yesterday's Hero was ELP's first release in CD format.

Yesterday's Hero

Track listing

1. You've Gotta Believe

(Lake)

2. Bach Before the Mast

(George Malcolm; arranged by Emerson)

3. Haunted

(Emerson, Lake)

4. Retribution Drive

(Lake)

5. Yancey Special

(Meade Lux Lewis; arranged by Emerson)

6. Fire in Your Eyes

(Lake)

7. I Don't Know Why

(Lake)

8. Night Chase

(Emerson)

9. Slave to Love

(Lake)

10. Peter Gunn (live)

(Henry Mancini; arranged by Emerson, Lake, Palmer)

Greg. No, this isn't my solo album, it is ELP of course. Yes, there are a lot of my compositions on the record, but I am in the band, right? Despite what one thinks, the tunes still had to pass band muster, just as we've always done from the very beginning. [Asked about the apparent absence of Keith compositions] I'm happy to talk about any of the songs on the new album, you?

Greg. Why sure, I understand that more than a few fans are wondering where the classic ELP sound went, the progressive aspect if you want to call it that. They have to remember that the ELP sound, for lack of a better term, is the proper balance of the three individuals. Do things sometimes get out of balance? Maybe they do for a song, or series of songs; but this is a rather simplistic view. The band serves to present the song or songs, which is what we did here. I'm very pleased that some mainstream critics find a few of the new songs a welcome change from the usual approach ELP is known for. I mean, we're not the only progressive band that has done something like this.

Greg. ELP is absolutely still a functioning recording and touring entity, guaranteed. I promise you there will be more original ELP music to come; it's a definite maybe, although I'm extremely non-committal. Not to worry, ELP has plenty of ideas left.

Carl. Keith is all over the record, can't you tell? I certainly can, and without Keith there is no ELP, and this is an ELP record. I mean, did you listen to the Malcolm piece [editor – George Malcolm, Bach Before the Mast]? It is an absolutely, genuine Keith tour de force with the piano and harpsichord firing on all cylinders; it actually reminds me a bit of Tank in that regard. But right now Keith is probably at home and by a piano. He is always just a phone call away from Greg and me.

Carl. Greg's tunes are wonderful songs with nice melodies, lovely arrangements. What's not to like?

Greg. I think our most vocal critics hate us for how our music affects them, as such. If I had to guess, it's that ELP's music, that is ELP's original music, much of it but not all, it interrupts their comfort zone; the predictability as it were. I mean, in music we are geared to the anticipation of resolution, omitting frequencies and delaying resolutions or introducing a new or varied theme causes unease. What ELP excelled at was frustrating these harmonic expectations or musical structures; this was intriguing to many and caught the attention of listeners, which in turn drew them to ELP and others too, of course, who were also despised. When they do hear something that could be interpreted as more conventional, there is this confusion it seems. This unusual approach requires attentive listening and analysis, something which may have been too much for people mesmerized by three minutes of crash and burn, which I can appreciate on occasion as well. So, ELP finds itself in this conundrum, when we create music which can be labeled progressive or futurist, we receive ire, then when we do something more mainstream we're not seen as credible. It's actually rather amusing.

122

[Greg and Carl interviewed together]

Greg. Did we know what Keith was up to? How about you? I have no idea. I didn't even see him on stage last tour. What about you?

Carl. He was there; didn't you see him selling t-shirts?

Greg. That's right, that's right, yes. Bootleg t-shirts, the ones that fall apart after one wash, and of course overcharging people, four bob a shirt in his pocket. Have you seen him?

Carl. Who?

Greg. Keith?

Carl. Keith who?

Greg. That's what I was going to ask you.

Carl. What does he look like?

Greg. Shady character.

Carl. Carries knives, does he?

Greg. Not all the time.

Carl. I know him; he tried to get me to join the Army.

Greg. Nasty piece of work, that one.

Carl. He likes Italians.

Greg. We all do, that doesn't help.

Carl. Tell me again who were we looking for...Gladstone?

Greg. I tell you what; if you see him, have him give me a ring, preferably after Christmas.

[Interview ends]

Greg. Some interviewers as well as fans have asked if the album title is a reference to ELP being former carriers of the progressive torch, and no, that wasn't consciously done. It was within the context of one song, the story of the song. I tell you, the insight of our fans is an amazing thing, they seem to tune into subtle points I can't even think of.

Greg. It's certainly very gratifying when one of your songs is revisited, not just seasonally but also in the charts. I thought that might happen with Fanfare [editor – Fanfare for the Common Man] but to see it with [I Believe in] Father Christmas, it's very rewarding, rewarding that a segment of the public is sharing a celebration of the Christmas season with your song.

Carl. Of course, we have the same critics hounding us that the record company purposely pushed Father Christmas in the wake of Yesterday's Hero not performing as expected, or did we – or they – expect it? I mean, it just barely scraped in, if it got to number #5, sure...maybe? But what can you say to someone who is that intent on just kicking us around? Is the record company using ELP to battle pop artists for the top of the charts? If you don't like the band, fine, but at least think things through just a bit.

Greg. We don't have a need to promote this new record in extremis, and considering how much touring we've always done throughout our career, this shouldn't come as a total surprise. We do of course have a substantial back catalog that we can tour on, but we always try to balance the shows with a regard for the past and to present what's new. We will undoubtedly be recording and touring in the future.

Carl. We didn't think it was necessary to tour in support of the record this time. We've had an exceptional run since the debut, and it's not unusual for bands to regroup and reflect; it's quite a natural thing actually. No disaster has befallen any of us, we're simply going to reorient ourselves and refocus.

Keith. As the composer of the more extended pieces for ELP incorporating different styles, I've been asked more than once if the band was ever concerned about becoming the victim, if that's the right word, of my ambitions and if that was the reason for doing Murderrock. [Pauses] No, I mean, throughout the band's history all three of us have made various suggestions regarding production or a particular album's presentation as it relates to the concept or content, but Greg and Carl were always supportive of me pushing the boundaries between rock and classical and jazz, and that was all I really asked for. If anything, I could see that as an accusation worthy of pursuit regarding my position towards the end of The Nice where I simply became the dominant, but I won't say indispensable, figure. Unlike some bands where the composing team loses interest or friction develops, Greg and I maintained our ability to write as a team, with Carl on occasion too, of course. We consciously worked on this with the debut and Tarkus to ensure we had an understanding of each other, and this bore fruit with how they were accepted, and it sustains itself to this day.

Keith. While doing the soundtrack work, I found myself exploring elements of different musical styles, world music and such, and I really tried to determine why progressive rock, art rock, or whatever you'd like to call it, received such tremendous disdain; a disdain that continues to this day. I know it might not be a popular view, but I think progressive rock is the victim of a gatekeeper mentality of a particular doctrine or ideology. You could say this about the free jazz style as well. It's seen as elitist or classist, and unlike the more primitive rock elements which are celebrated or deemed superior, we don't despise ourselves or our history. I assure you, we grew up just as poor as any of these outliers for whatever their excuse is. I just couldn't see music being part of the class war other than it was perhaps media manufactured.

Keith. When punk showed up and ELP and other legacy acts were being knocked as tired, old farts, I really think they missed the potential from a musical perspective. I mean, as young lads you all wind up doing the same excesses, right? But punk seemed to pride itself on flaunting an inability to be musically proficient, and at the same time missed the possibility of using harmonic aggression as a way to, I don't know, lash out more broadly I suppose. This is not something new at all. Indian ragas and African polyrhythms have effects on us,

125

just as modal music. Had they studied the repetition of sounds as it related to primitive rock, I think they could have been a lot more impactful musically. I also think that there was an element in punk that didn't just only despise the larger, established acts such as ELP; I think they were rebelling against the status quo, in general. I don't know, at the end of the day they were still hilarious.

Keith. With all this negativity directed towards us, it's as if the critics saw progressive rock as part of a hostile world they rejected and a fan base that, in turn, rejected them. Then the reviews just continued to become more vicious and ghastly. We sought to celebrate our musical heritage which is vast and rich, so we're not going to spit on our past. If punk was supposedly a media driven healing response to the excesses of progressive rock, then I think you'd have the world's greatest case for malpractice. I'm proud of the contributions we've made to the rock canon in the context of the progressive arena and with the other artists we are associated with there, and we did it organically and purely on a musical level.

Keith. I sat down with a journalist recently who has had a history of being a bit contentious with ELP, you know, the insults, the whole bit. But, he seemed to be approachable and a rather bright guy, so I wanted to see if we could talk things out. I asked him if he agreed that music is a reflection of people, culture, and we, that is ELP, touch a segment of the listening public. Isn't that validation that our music is helping them define themselves as part of the greater culture? He agreed to an extent, but he felt that ELP seemed to be focusing on showing off, that it wasn't genuine. He said that the music, I imagine he meant rock, when it's broken down to its purest or basic elements it can then only have the depth of sincerity he was looking for. I asked him if had seen some of the rather crass, but also humorous to a degree, lyrics of the bands he was touting and what that was a reflection of. He advised he was aware, and that it was all part of the experience, if you will. When I told him that a great number of our fans do not see the sincerity in purposely trying to prevent music, or art, or technology, from advancing or progressing and that skill or mastery should be lauded and appreciated. After all, in a broader sense, when you go to the Doctor, would you

126

like them not to use the latest and greatest treatments and techniques, or perhaps would you find it ridiculous to watch a movie with 30-year old crude special effects; wouldn't you want people in any field to be engaged in pursuing proper and advanced training and techniques? He sniffed and told me, and I'm not joking here, "Now you're just being an elitist because you can afford it all."

Keith. While working on Murderrock, I found myself looking back at my development as a composer and arranger, specifically using the Moog as a sort of brass replicator at times, if you will, and where that came from. I really didn't have that opportunity with The Nice. But then, upon getting the Moog, experimenting with all its capabilities and the sounds helped me remember stories told by older relatives of all these wonderful brass bands that were all over Britain at one time. This was probably in the mid to late 1800's I think, I'm not positive. But, these bands sprung up not only for entertainment, but they were a source of local pride, you know, much like the football team of the town or area. This was a community at work, working class mostly, not necessarily professional musicians. I did some research and found out Lancashire was quite active when it came to this brass band movement. I imagine this grew because it was promoted and seen as somewhat respectable, and, I mean, after all, you have to keep the rabble in check and distracted, you know [laughs], make sure they're entertained and don't have them read too much. So, I do think that was part of my subconscious musical upbringing, you know.

Keith. Here we are in the '80's and with the leap forward in synth technology, you have all these amazing sounds, you know, readily available at the push of a button. Nowadays, there's the one guy standing on one leg and holding down a note, looking very dramatic and such, and all of a sudden it's considered real or relevant. But, then with ELP's keyboard centric music and the use of the synthesizer, it's seen as misguided or that it doesn't belong, out of touch or out of date. It's sort of like the clarinet or the saxophone, there's this instant reaction of, ah, that's jazz! Synths in this modern pop style are seen as technically and stylistically suitable, but we're seen as boorish or even provincial. I was mocked for coaxing all these unconventional sounds from the Moog, and I had those accusations leveled at me in the early '70s, especially after Tarkus, while someone like Pete Townsend was lauded for using synths appropriately, more as an effect, and with great skill as sound sculpting rather than technique. I've resigned myself to the fact that we could do no right with the critics; perhaps we even scared some of them. But we've stuck to our guns, and not necessarily to our commercial detriment, not at all.

Chapter Eight

Touch and Go, 1986-1987

The Regathering

Emerson, Lake, and Palmer

The Alternate History

1975-2000

1985 was a year of reflection and reorganization for ELP as Keith emerged from his semi-seclusion to only briefly mention and discuss his work on Murderrock, movie soundtrack work in general, the unexpected vacation, as well as his confirmation that he still sees ELP as the major outlet for his work. Greg and Carl make no reference to what seems to have been Keith's unofficial, semi-sabbatical from ELP and focus solely on what lies ahead for the band as a whole. The band reconvenes in March 1986 to record their new album – Touch and Go – which is released in September. There seems to be a conscious effort to reestablish and reconnect with the ELP reputation with an acknowledgement and return to progressive style, sound, and lyrical content. Touch and Go, the album's first single, peaks at US #60; in their homeland it does not chart. However, I Believe in Father Christmas once again briefly enters the charts at UK #98. The album's second single, Lay Down Your Guns, does not chart on either side of the Atlantic. To further acknowledge a return to progressive form, the band takes advantage of the technological advances in MIDI [editor – Musical Instrumental Digital

Interface] and brings back Abaddon's Bolero into the set as the opening number after it had been briefly attempted in 1972. At the time it was forever dropped from the live set due to the then primitive equipment limitations. The band commences with an international tour in October 1986.

Touch and Go

Track listing

1. The Score

(Emerson, Lake)

2. Learning to Fly

(Emerson, Lake)

3. The Miracle

(Emerson, Lake)

4. Touch and Go

(Emerson, Lake)

5. Love Blind

(Emerson, Lake)

6. Step Aside

(Emerson, Lake)

7. Lay Down Your Guns

(Emerson, Lake, Steve Gould)

8. Vacant Possession

(Emerson, Lake, Palmer)

Keith.   I've had some people ask me if 1984 and 1985 were lost years for me [pauses] or for the band. No...I don't believe so, no...no. Greg and Carl aren't shy, and were true to their word regarding my temporary excursion. And also, I've had many moments of self-reflection over the years. I always wonder if I'm doing the right thing with my music, even going back to The Three Fates, Tarkus, all the orchestral ideas I've had, the arrangements of standards and such. I've lost track of how many compositions start out with an orchestral foundation and are then pared back, and vice versa as well. This is something many composers do in hindsight, even with all the positive encouragement in the world. Also, I'm aware that Greg and Carl have a rightful expectation of the music I bring forward, what I am committed to, and for that reason I always go back to what is dearest to my heart, which is ELP.

Keith.   The offer to do the Murderrock soundtrack was another one of those moments; I felt a calling to do this, much the same as in 1975 with my piano pieces. I actually crossed paths with Cozy Powell [editor – English drummer] in late 1984 or 1985 after things were calming down. I've actually known him for some time, he has quite a nice farm in Berkshire. I told him what I had done and was expressing some regret. He told me that as an artist, as long as you're not being deceptive or leaving people in the lurch, follow what you want to do. He said, look at my career, I've bounced around and done everything I could do, and it's been great all the way from the Sorcerers in the 1960's to Whitesnake and everything in between [editor – Powell's discography during that time includes The Jeff Beck Group, Rainbow, and The Michael Schenker Group]. That was very encouraging, but it really all would have been for nothing had it not been for Greg and Carl who were unfailingly kind and supportive; their regular phone calls and reassurances heartened me when it seems I had disappeared or when doubt was creeping in. Not many bands, of any stature really, would have put up with this.
131

At first I wasn't sure about it, but I think they've grown to know me better than I know myself, that probably made the difference.

Keith. I can still recall clearly that after Greg and I composed Trilogy the song, I felt we had reached a stage where we knew where the other was going in regards to composition when we worked together. It was rather uncanny, really. With the Touch and Go record I feel like we reached another plateau in that way, but it's difficult to describe. It's rather like a deeper level of knowledge; maybe one could call it intuition, what the other half brings to the table. I mention that because with Trilogy, as a purely composed piece, I realized I truly had left The Nice behind. But I should add, I don't mean that in a negative way. The debut was a step towards that feeling, as was Tarkus, but Trilogy completely solidified it. I mention this because with this record it's like we are again at another stratum. I feel a bit of similarity with Trilogy and The Miracle as they both have a Liszt [editor – Franz Liszt, German composer] influence as far as they are, to me, symphonic poems with other classical nods. You know, a Neapolitan chord or a French sixth. While not as sweeping as some of ELP's epic pieces of the past, I believe it is one our finest works. I also was quite surprised to hear that Father Christmas entered the UK charts in 1984 and again this past year [editor - 1986]. Maybe our fans felt a bit sorry for us after what we went through [laughs], please don't, please, no...we have been and continue to be very fortunate. But really, the people at the record company certainly got it right when they believed that the appeal and quality of that song will lend itself to being a perpetual seasonal favorite, so it's not a complete surprise, but quite pleasing to see it actually happen.

Greg. We were not tempted to go down this purely commercial route many of our contemporaries have chosen, some with great success. I know many of those guys, and I'm very happy for them. But we wanted to stay true to our progressive roots, continuing to push the concept of European based music but with the addition of Keith really digging into the technology, but then not losing sight or focus of the ELP sound. I've been asked about the lack of a trademark acoustic track, but the songs developed as they did. While it has become an expected feature, an acoustic number, remember that I didn't have one on Tarkus. The focus really is just on presenting some great songs without automatically tossing something in, a classical adaptation or an acoustic track, simply because that's what's expected. It's quite the balancing act to deliver a well-paced album you know; it can be a bit tricky.

Carl. I do have some compositional ideas, but with the material Keith and Greg have been bringing forward, it's nothing that is too sympathetic with what the band is currently creating, my material will eventually see the light of day, I'm not worried. As I've mentioned before, I didn't have any writing credits on Brain Salad Surgery, which certainly wasn't to that album's detriment. We are mostly concerned that we have a dynamic and coherent piece of work to present.

Keith. I can't think of any of my progressive contemporaries, well, English keyboard players anyway, that aren't aware of or influenced by Vaughn Williams [editor – UK], who was an incredible composer. Touch and Go is based on his arrangement of Greensleeves which uses the English folk song Lovely Joan which works so well in a dramatic, symphonic setting, you know, a minor key and all. Being English, I was really drawn to him as he forged a path for English composers breaking from the German tradition and really looked at England's own musical heritage, which is actually pretty extensive if not very well known, sadly.

Keith. What's interesting is that Williams formed a friendship with Gustav Holst [editor – English composer and arranger], and I think it was Greg that did Mars [editor – Mars, The Bringer of War, the first movement of Holst's orchestral suite The Planets] in [King[Crimson. His output was incredible, and he also really was a man's man, I think he drove an ambulance in World War 1. Much like ELP, he worked to bring music of quality to the regular people; it wasn't an aspect of snobbery just like we're accused of. It really is a desire to bring forward the melody of the movement, of symphonic or classical or progressive rock, whatever we are destined to be labeled or described as.

Keith. I don't believe credit was necessary [editor – referring to Touch and Go, the song], we know that we've ran into that before going all the way back to the debut. You know the story...yes, oh, hello Mrs. Bartok, so very sorry about that.

133

Some of you also may have recognized some Vaughn Williams' influence in Con Fuoco [editor – Toccata Con Fuoco from the Pirates album] as well. Most Americans don't know, and many British probably don't remember, anymore, that Williams wrote a lovely piece called Thanksgiving for Victory. Those of us who are World War 2 children or had war parents or grandparents, this has a lot of meaning, national significance to me, to us.

Greg. When Keith brought in the Touch and Go theme and explained to me its origins with Vaughn Williams, I did some research as I always enjoy doing. I was surprised to see that Williams studied with Parry [editor – Hubert Parry, British composer and music educator] who co-wrote Jerusalem. Seeing this and looking back at our own work, it gave me a sense of pride in recognizing ELP, in however minor a role or footnote, is inevitably worming its way into the British music lineage.

Greg. I understand some rock fans and the usual groups of critics – our biggest fans – are saying we're a bit disingenuous when we're saying that the commercial approach is not for ELP especially after the Yesterday's Hero record. But, it was a moment in time, ELP's time, where it occurred organically; that is, we didn't sit around and conceive of a commercial album. Circumstances in ELP at that moment in time dictated the path, if you will. There have been other times in the band's history where the alarms were going off that maybe we were headed off course and had to reorient ourselves, with Winter's Light or maybe even the early days of Tarkus for example. But at the end of the day, it is ELP...it is all ELP.

Carl. The Touch and Go record was a bit of a temptation to venture into electronic drums, something that I was a pioneer in with Brain Salad Surgery as you know. We all know that Graeme with the Moodies [editor – Edge, Moody Blues drummer] was the first to use an electronic drum device, and then of course you had Simmons [editor – British manufacturer of electronic drums] starting in 1981 or so. But, at this time I don't see myself ever going fully electric no matter how good these kits can become, and I believe they eventually will become very, very good. I see it as a supplement to the classic kit. But, we're not trend chasers, never have been. We'll investigate and pursue technology if necessary or if it suits where we are regarding writing, recording, or for production as we're getting ready to go on tour. We have an army of boffins constantly on the prowl that keep Keith, Greg, and myself aware of instrumental or technical developments that would be of interest or beneficial to us.

Keith. A classical adaptation or adaptations? Yes, we're known for it, and embrace it, absolutely. Well, but not this time. I mean, I'm sure there will be more of that in the future, I know there will be. I have some ideas, I just need to, shall we say, convince the others. But we had such strong material for this album, why do something, you know, cliché like, I don't know, Toccata and Fugue or Clair de Lune just for the sake of checking the box.

Keith. Since you're asking, while there is no outright classical adaptation, I really couldn't help myself and had to throw in a snippet, however minor, it's part of my and the legacy of ELP to give a classical nod whenever we can. You're keen on this it seems, were you able to find it? [Interviewer replies in the negative]. Well, here you go then. In Learning to Fly there's a brief introduction to the instrumental section which comes from Bartok's [editor – Bela Bartok, Hungarian composer] Divertimento, the rhythm is not identical, but there it is.

Greg. I actually had a fan write me a very nice letter where he laid out this wide-ranging story of how the spectre reference in Knife Edge is the same character reference in The Miracle and that it ties in with the story lines of Tarkus and Karn Evil 9. I mean, this was an expansive, very impressive piece of work, mind-blowing actually, dissecting all the lyrics with incredible detail and referencing documented history, secret societies, conspiracies. I do love history myself of course. I actually wrote him back and told him how flattering it was that our music motivated him to do this creative thinking. I encouraged him to do some original writing of his own. It has motivated me also, as a lyricist, to further explore unconscious streams or themes in my writings based on my own long and short term interests that I can apply in the future.

Greg. Another bit of Bartok, right? The thing with Keith's compositions, even the
135

shorter ones that are more song oriented, Keith throws in so much, all these sly little bits and pieces a contemporary composer wouldn't think of, or wouldn't be aware of. There are many, many quotes and bits from Keith all throughout the ELP catalog that most, except the hard-core music enthusiasts aren't even aware of. When performing live, due to the spontaneous nature of improvisation, this is done even more so.

Carl. I don't think the absence of a classical adaptation hurts the release or us as a band. We've done plenty and I'm sure there will be more. If anything, The Miracle can justifiably be considered a classical piece with its very strong, dramatic, symphonic overtones and in structure and form. I'm surprised that more fans have not picked up on what an interesting composition Keith came up with. I understand that Greg's very descriptive and picturesque lyrics grab one's attention, but listen to the shifts and changes structurally and harmonically, it's a fantastic piece.

Carl. When Keith brought up that he snuck in the Bartok segment in Learning to Fly we gave him a proper twisting, [laughs] didn't he learn anything from recording The Barbarian [editor- from the eponymous Emerson, Lake, and Palmer debut album]?

Keith. Well, yes, that's very keen of you to pick up that the sequenced part for the beginning of The Score as a sort of homage to the famous Moog sequence for Welcome Back [editor – Karn Evil 9, First Impression, Part Two]. Is it that obvious [laughs]? Very good, very perceptive of you, you're picking up on all my secrets. How much do you charge to keep a secret [laughs]? I try not to be too sentimental with my music but every now and then, and as I get a bit older, I can't help myself.

Greg. I don't think it's particularly distasteful or offensive to reference one's own works provided it's done with balance and of course, it must be done with respect to the listener as well. I imagine a part of it is in the timing, where in the band's history this is being done, right? An obvious reference is at least honest, it's not like some bands where they just move some chords from one of their own hits

136

and try to sell it again. We wouldn't, and we won't, be like some bands where all the songs sound the same, perhaps due to their genre or simple instrumentation. We're taking the fans on a journey, and sometimes you look back together where we've been.

Greg. We were quite surprised when the record company advised us that [I Believe in] Father Christmas crept onto the charts again. When it was first released, there was some talk in the industry that it could become a seasonal favorite. But, one doesn't know at the time, it's never a guarantee. We actually have experienced this before with Lucky Man, if I recall it entered the charts twice in America, propelled along by the great inertia we had there in the early '70's [editor – Lucky Man charted US #48 in 1971, and US #51 in 1972]. One just trusts and assumes it's the record company professionals knowing their jobs and doing the necessary promoting. They have been proven somewhat right, with that particular song over the past 10 years with ELP. And of course we're very grateful, but it's also a bit, maybe awkward, but not in an unpleasant way. It's like an extended applause, very much cherished, and you strive to be a bit humble about it.

Carl. We had discussed that it was important for us that the opening track for the Touch and Go record [editor – The Score] would have to have a few of the ELP trademarks, something out of the chute for people that maybe had doubts about the band after the Yesterday's Hero record, you know? So, Keith does his keyboard bits, I'm sure it's plain to hear, and Greg has some obvious lyrical references as well. For myself, I do my trademark fanfare shuffle as we now call it [editor – referencing Fanfare for the Common Man]; time and time again, it works quite well for ELP.

Carl. I don't think there's anything tasteless about making a compositional or performance reference or two to the work one has done in the past provided it's done with enough subtlety and skill. I thought we did it quite well by keeping in mind these pieces or elements of ELP's legacy and history that are meaningful to the fans and to us. Was it solely due to the response from the previous record?

Well, I think it's obvious there is an attempt at an obvious reconnection, a reaffirmation of sorts. If we were stealing another artist blind I could see that as being offensive and rightly so, but we're stealing from ourselves, [laughs] if that's possible.

Keith. When creating the set, and considering that we had been out of the public eye for the better part of a year, we looked back at maybe something that we may have attempted during the very early years, but were limited by technology. We all, mostly, agreed upon Abaddon's Bolero.

Greg. The Bolero is popular with the fans, but unfortunately when we tried it in, I think it was 1972, after Trilogy, it was a bit of a mess. When preparing to hit the road after the record was released, we realized we had painted ourselves into a corner with all the overdubs. It sounded wonderful in the studio, but we got carried away with the advancements in recording technology at the time, so the overdubs on many tracks were unending, and the Bolero was no different. We tried some shenanigans with the Mellotron [editor – created in England in 1963, an electro-mechanical keyboard utilizing sounds recorded on audio tape], some bass pedals, and a Revox [editor – tape recorder]. But, as is typical with untried, groundbreaking technology, it was a dog's breakfast. We had a bit of a shouting match after the show, and never attempted it again. But now, with the advent of MIDI in the hands of someone like Keith, we can absolutely make it work, and work quite well.

Carl. What MIDI offers a band like ELP in a live setting is quite nice, but we're not going to just create waterfalls of sound because we can. Keith is especially sensitive to the fact that he wants to play what is being heard, and when people come to see ELP in concert, that's what they want and what they get. Some bands you see these days have an extra keyboard player tucked away behind or under the stage, and even some guitar-oriented bands – I won't say which ones – are doing the same thing to fatten up the sound. I did mention to Keith that the Bolero isn't in 3/4, and that it's a march; he said perhaps it is, but [laughs] that would be a dreadful sounding title!

138

Keith. The proposition of touring in quad for this tour was our way of saying, or one of our ways, is that we haven't gone anywhere, we're still the same band we were back in 1973 or 1974. We treat our reputation seriously, and after having a relatively low profile for a couple of years, we wanted to make a bit of a splash of sorts live. We didn't want to do something daft or out of character, just something extra for our audience.

Greg. With the advancement of technology, touring in quad gives us the opportunity to especially showcase the sounds Keith is able to pull up. The GX-1 [editor – Yamaha synthesizer] especially has a very unique stereo presentation, and of course the modern synths are simply a step beyond the Hammond and Moog in fidelity, but perhaps not as dangerous, if that's the right word.

Carl. It's a fine line between doing something a bit special or revisiting something unique, but yet not appear to be desperate of begging to be seen, if you will. We knew that after the Yesterday's Hero record and then regrouping in 1985 we wanted to do something extra when it came to playing live. Obviously with quad, Keith's sounds will be front and center, but I'll certainly be exploring some electronic possibilities as well. I've been there before, you know.

Keith. We did at one point consider a concept piece using the combined music that eventually became The Score and The Miracle as well as Touch and Go. The Score would have been scaled back from the song it became to using the parts excluding the verses, and it probably would have had a reprise section, the others also, maybe. But, as the lyrical parts came together, they did develop as individual songs. We've done something like that before where we considered using Hoedown as a prelude to The Sheriff [editor – both from ELP's album Trilogy], but in rehearsal and planning out the album, these things are sometimes only discussed in passing and then put aside.

Greg. I thought it was important that we bridge that chasm between doing something uniquely ELP but not appear to be too on the nose, you know? I mean, if we would have come back and done two concept pieces, I think it would appear that we were trying a bit too hard. Instead, we dished up the classic ELP approach in a more refined and natural way.

Carl. Returning from a relative low point, which ELP had never before experienced, with a sense of standing is a difficult thing to do; there is a tremendous amount of second-guessing going on. We had considered different options and approaches. Do we create an extended suite, do we focus on a more contemporary approach which some of our peers have done quite well. Do we force the issue, or do we simply follow the creative process? As it turned out, the songs all developed quite naturally as they were presented. Keith and Greg came very prepared with the material; there wasn't a lot of deviation. It was very gratifying to see the album do well in Japan [editor – JP #19]; it was as if the very dedicated fans we have there let it known they were satisfied to see ELP come back with all the features they've come to expect.

Carl. Somebody pointed out to me that the cover is actually a modern, art-deco version of Trilogy. We really hadn't thought about that, but, there is no doubt there's an obvious but perhaps accidental connection. I imagine this is what happens over the course of a lengthy career when there's the possibility that someone in the art department probably wasn't aware that we've had a career going back 16 years.

Chapter Nine

Conquering Tide, 1988

Atlantic Records 40th Anniversary Celebration

Emerson, Lake, and Palmer

The Alternate History

1975-2000

The Touch and Go tour goes through March 1987 and sees ELP playing a somewhat condensed US show schedule, but they ensure that the UK, Europe, and Japan get a fair amount of shows before the tour's end. The band goes into the studio in September but is unable to decide on the album's direction. ELP reenters the studio in March 1988 and begin writing and recording material. In April, ELP are invited to play at Atlantic Records' 40th Anniversary Celebration to be held in May. ELP play Lucky Man, Karn Evil 9, First Impression, Part Two, and Fanfare for the Common Man. In July 1988, ELP release their new album, Conquering Tide. The corner piece of the album is an extended concept piece which – once again for ELP – deals with maritime and historical themes, but one that is explicitly British in nature. This time, the story details the English defeat of the Spanish Armada in 1588 (a coincidental 400th anniversary) which allows Greg to lyrically showcase his known love of history. In a first for ELP, Keith is the sole contributor of music and lyrics on an ELP track with On My Way Home, a personal dedication to his former manager of The Nice, Tony Stratton-Smith, who passed away in early 1987. On My Way Home is released as a single, but does not chart; the Conquering Tide tour commences in August.

Conquering Tide

Track listing

1. Conquering Tide

a. Threatening Storm

(Emerson)

b. Ocean's Border

(Emerson, Lake)

c. Hellburners

(Emerson, Palmer)

d. Triumph

(Emerson, Lake)

e. Tapestry

(Emerson)

2. Love Under Fire

(Emerson, Lake)

3. Blue Light

(Emerson, Lake)

4. Dream Runner

(Emerson)

5. Street War

(Emerson, Lake)

6. On My Way Home

(Emerson)

Keith. We had a bit of a false start with the Conquering Tide record; it reminded me a bit of what we went through with Tarkus. Not that it was to that degree of disagreement, but we had to sort out the direction. I was strongly suggesting that in light of the Touch and Go album and the unofficial break we had prior, it had been more than a few years and that we owed the fans an extended piece. Whenever we interact with the fans in any way, it is the most popular request we receive, please do an epic, conceptual piece.

Greg. We tested each other a bit when we first went into the studio, Keith presented the case for an extended piece, but the theme hadn't been sorted out. I am all for the broad and sweeping pieces we're known for, but there has to be a coherent theme. Quite frankly, Keith had the music, but we didn't have even a basic idea of the theme, and I wasn't content to simply throw something together. We have a standard to meet.

Carl. As the observer of the two composers, I've seen the growth between Keith and Greg since the debut. Whereas in the beginning the question of the album's direction could have resulted in ultimatums and the like, with this record it was more like, "Look, let's take a step back, think it over, and then regroup." Which is exactly what we did; the bumps were smoothed over, and we all went back to work.

Keith. Atlantic Record's 40th Anniversary show was wonderful to be part of; it was
143

a true, historical event. To say that they have been an integral part of our career would be a massive, massive understatement. It's also important to remember, for ourselves and the greater progressive fan base, that we are part of a greater industry. There might be genres that I don't particularly follow or that our fans don't really care for, but these are very successful and talented people in their own way that have contributed greatly not only to the success of Atlantic Records, but to popular music in general.

Greg. The organizers of Atlantic's 'It's Only Rock and Roll' celebration initially had scheduled us to play before The Bee Gees. The Bee Gees are a fine group, but when we looked at other bands playing, what were they thinking? So, we knocked on Stewart's [editor – Stewart Young, ELP manager] door who convinced the organizers to reconsider scheduling us closer to Yes or Genesis, maybe even Foreigner. It's a pity I wouldn't get a chance to see Ian [editor – Ian McDonald, original King Crimson multi-instrumentalist and then Foreigner keyboard, woodwinds, and guitar player] either way. Eventually, as we all know now, we wound up playing right before Yes, which was much more appropriate, better flowing for the show.

Greg. With these types of large, sprawling events you're unfortunately at the mercy of the organizer's talent with everything, the overall organization, the sound, the monitors, and the stage arrangement. There's so much variation between what artists need to feel comfortable on stage. Thankfully it was done at a high level, unsurprisingly not quite at ELP's level, but still quite good. I must admit it was wonderful seeing groups like The Coasters and The Spinners perform and representing the early days of rock and roll, these are truly timeless songs and wonderful singers. It would be nice if one day there was some wide-ranging history of rock concert or series of concerts to highlight other well-deserving artists like Smokey Robinson.

Carl. These types of industry or historical shows certainly are a career highpoint; a time of reflection, a nice break from the routine, and obviously provide ample servings of all sorts of music for the fans. I mean, the show lasted something like

11 or 12 hours [editor – 13 hours], or as someone at the show remarked, an abbreviated Grateful Dead soundcheck [laughs]. I personally was thrilled to meet and see Mark [editor – Mark Steyn, keyboardist and vocalist] from Vanilla Fudge perform. It was quite nice to hear that he thinks the world of ELP.

Keith. So, we, all of us really, at the end of the day just can't stop being British [laughs], or maybe we just can't stop egging each other to be more British. Pirates, Memoirs, [For] Those Who Dare, and now Conquering Tide all are quite Anglophile. One of the things I regret, in hindsight, was not insisting in making Pirates identifiable enough. I didn't write the lyrics of course, and it's more presumed I suppose; having said that, it still is very good. Carl, by virtue of being in Tenerife, brought up some Spanish history, the typical tales of galleons, the armada, gold...which got Greg's attention and ire, good-natured of course. He was rather adamant that the story ultimately would be told from a British perspective.

Keith. Starting with the Touch and Go and now into Conquering Tide, the technological advances have really been ramping up at an amazing pace. But you know, I'm not going to start reading raw MIDI data, there's no time, and I'm really not sold on the idea of combining digital and analog, not yet anyway. ELP has some fabulous technicians that know much more about the developing technology than I do, or I should say, than we do. At the end of the day, the tune or the melody carries the piece, regardless of the technology.

Greg. Sometimes things just work out with one's interest and one's art. One of my prized possessions is a very old copy of manuscript. I want you to get ready for the title because it makes our instrumental song title Apple Blossoms [editor – When the Apple Blossoms Bloom in the Windmills of Your Mind, I'll Be Your Valentine] seem like a puff of smoke. Here you go: The Spanish Armada in 1588, and the tapestry hangings of the House of Lords representing the several engagements between the English and Spanish Fleets. [Pause] Did you get that? [Laughs] It is a wonderful and thoroughly British overview, from the time, following the defeat of the Spanish Armada. It is related and presented with classic Brit' stoicism and understatement with magnificent details, charts, maps, and the like. It is an amazing piece of work considering the times it was done.

Carl. I shared with Greg my idea of a sort of Pirates, part two, but maybe from a national perspective, and I had mentioned Spanish. Greg liked it and mentioned that while Pirates was very good, the narrative perspective was never really clear, or at least not obvious. He then took the idea and used the British point of view. I imagine it would have seemed a bit disingenuous pretending we're conquistadors of the sea considering ELP always has been unapologetically British.

Keith. On My Way Home is, of course, dedicated to Tony Stratton-Smith, the former manager of The Nice. He passed away last year from cancer, it's so unbelievably sad. Despite what people may think, I was 100% genuine. I know the naysayers look for any chance to beat ELP down if they sense we're trying to be too clever. Strat, as many knew him, had a great business sense and was a terrific promoter; he cared for his artists, personally and professionally. Greg was very kind and supportive once I told him I had an idea for a song and had some lyrics. We almost had an amusing mix-up on the liner notes with On My Way Home similar to what happened to Karn Evil 9 for the First Impression, where the credits confusingly labeled Emerson vocals, written by Lake, or something similar. This time, the pre-release notes showed music and vocals by Emerson…goodness, no. Somebody commented back when that happened with those confusing Karn Evil 9 vocal credits, they said KE, meaning me I suppose, nein! [Laughs] Doing the computer voice of the muse on Karn Evil 9 is the closest I'll ever come to singing, if you can call it that, on an ELP recording.

Greg. I thought Keith did a fine job with the music and the lyrics for On My Home. It is a sincere, emotional outpouring over Tony [editor – Tony Stratton-Smith], and I see it as very honest and I had no problem at all singing it. For Carl and me, we realize that without Tony watching out for and over Keith during those very wild and early years, there very well may never have been an ELP.

Carl. On My Way Home is an interesting dynamic for ELP, Greg singing Keith's lyrics. This is something I wouldn't have even guessed as a possibility even going
146

back several years or albums, but life and experiences can be powerful elements to bring about an event, not necessarily a complete change. It is a bit power ballad-like, which is not something that ELP is known for. Writing and recording it was very important to Keith, which I understand completely.

Keith. I'm not really a fan of labels, simply for the fact that for a band like ELP, what would you label us as? If you hear The Barbarian and then From the Beginning, what should we be categorized as? Are we progressive as, say, Pink Floyd, or is Pink Floyd more progressive than ELP? Certainly not the same instrumental style, I would say. Is ELP art rock, or symphonic rock?

Greg. Giving a band a category or label is a bit lazy, I think. I mean, categories have been around forever, so when you have a one-dimensional band, critics simply file it in a category; done. But with progressive bands, it becomes a bit more difficult, you know. With King Crimson we went from 21st Century Schizoid Man to I Talk to the Wind, from heavy rock to a pastoral tune. It's as if the critics can't let the fans decide, they slap on a label and let it loose. Of course, the progressive label has become a bit of a warning, you know, sort of like here's the leper, you'd better hide. I wonder if fans of mainstream contemporary music really thought that when they heard Lucky Man or From the Beginning, oh no, hold on, this is that progressive band, I can't listen to this. This is quite silly, enjoy the music.

Carl. I personally think ELP is simply too diverse to fit under one particular banner, it's just too eclectic. Someone will look at one piece and declare it fits under whatever style they feel like. Even if you were to say, right, well Tarkus and Karn Evil 9 are of one cloth, Pirates and Conquering Tide somewhat similar but again are of a slightly different type. Then of course you also have our instrumental pieces and Greg's acoustic-based songs. If there's anything that our music should be labeled, it would simply be European.

Keith. I was asked about maybe some uncomfortable similarities between Lay Down Your Guns and On My Way Home. But really, other than being piano-based, I really don't see it, they are sufficiently removed from each other. Of course,

147

lyrically it's chalk and cheese. If anything, Lay Down Your Guns is more of a straight-forward ballad whereas On My Way Home has more of the classically oriented accents and changes ELP fans are accustomed to in our signature pieces. It's more driving, almost march-like.

Greg. We've revisited certain themes before, you know? I mean, Pete and I revisited the demented circus-like atmosphere in Karn Evil 9 that he had explored before with King Crimson on the Lizard record, right? Karn Evil was on a global or universal scale, while Cirkus [editor – from King Crimson's Lizard album] was more personal, from what I know. Conquering Tide is similar to Pirates, but more identifiable on the level of a nation, in this case obviously being England. And, the story is sufficiently different I believe, rather than pillage and plunder it's one of national survival and resolve, the character. We just had to be a bit careful in not contradicting or drifting too far towards Memoirs or even Tarkus with its obvious anti-war or anti-violence theme, albeit different circumstances or conditions.

Carl. The thematic direction, if a piece calls for it, I leave that to Greg and Keith. There's no doubt that the scale of the music or the lyrical content can instrumentally drive the track to various levels of intensity, so it's my job to sense that and constantly provide that push-pull effect. When the entire band kicks in at certain points with an elevated zeal, you attain a sort of critical mass; the live improvisations of Aquatarkus and Fanfare [editor – Fanfare for the Common Man] and Rondo are good examples of that.

Chapter Ten

Landscape 19, 1989-1990

Emerson, Lake, and Palmer

The Alternate History

1975-2000

The Conquering Tide tour focuses on North America and Europe and lasts through February 1989. The band announces it will be taking the rest of the year off and that there will be a forthcoming announcement for ELP's 20th anniversary in 1990. As 1990 arrives, the record company keeps the band's profile aloft with the expected greatest hits and a career-spanning 20-year anniversary release, but surprisingly no tour is announced. Starting in June 1990, ELP fans once again notice a smattering of unusually named bands, seemingly with an obtuse or hidden ELP connection, being booked in smaller venues across the US. The band's management and the band members themselves admit as the tour starts that they are embarking on the second iteration of the incognito acoustic tour that they did back in 1980. The band advertises themselves randomly as Fillmore's Triumvirate, Landscape 19, Ham or Cheese, or Carl's Trousers.

Keith. We really felt we had an ELP-worthy concept with Conquering Tide, but as the shows went on we could sense a bit less enthusiasm. The response wasn't quite as flat as it was with Memoirs, and the Hellburners segment where Carl and

I work within its unusual time signature always seemed to get a good response. But, you know, the audience loves the classic material, how can you find that frustrating as an artist? It's something we're always eminently grateful for.

Greg. We used some quite dramatic backdrops for the Conquering Tide piece, panoramic views of the ocean and ships at sea; the audience seemed to be quite engaged. But we also recognized that it's very difficult to have the fans set aside their long-term favorites, Karn Evil, Pictures, maybe even Pirates, to make room for the new piece. How can you make someone cast aside a piece, or pieces, they've been listening to for 10 or 15 years? I mean, when I go see The Who, I might be interested in whatever new material they have to offer, but obviously I'm expecting to hear Baba O'Riley and Won't Get Fooled Again in all its glory.

Carl. Conquering Tide is vintage ELP, I'll always believe that. Was it our best? Probably not; was it our worst? In all honesty, I would say no; definitely not. But we are putting ourselves in a difficult, unwinnable situation; there is a lot of competition amongst the ELP concept pieces. Quite honestly, it's very likely that the classic ones will never be displaced or dethroned, ever. But, creating original music is what we do and will continue to do; we'll take it in stride however it may be received. I assure you that we worked just as hard on Conquering Tide as we did on the debut, Karn Evil or anything else we've done.

Keith. We considered touring in quad for Conquering Tide as we had done with the Touch and Go tour. And while it is quite nice, it is expensive to do these types of things. It also was a bit of a different time, after we had a break and we wanted to come on again at full gallop. But now that we have some consistency again, we explored other production enhancements.

Greg. We had done backdrops before, but with the advances in technology, we were really able to make it visually appealing. It was interesting seeing the audiences' different reactions to the visuals as we worked very hard to see it work in harmony with the music, the story. I've talked to other musicians, who have employed special effects live, and they all say that it is very tempting to be taken in by it all, lights, lasers and all, as you're in the middle of it and forget the job at hand.

Carl. All of us came up understanding the importance of production, seeing it emerge with the Beatles as pioneers with mixed media and such. With Arthur Brown I probably had the best and the worst of it, it was a bit over the top, even outlandish; I'm still paying the price today. But, it gets you recognized, no doubt. With ELP we really, really look at what will enhance the show to ensure it doesn't take on a life of its own, that it doesn't become superfluous.

Keith. Even after all these years, just when you think you've got it all figured out, I'm still experimenting and learning. On the Touch and Go tour I experimented with using the GX-1 a bit more on Tarkus rather than the Hammond, especially on the Eruption part, and like I did on Threatening Storm [editor – opening segment on Conquering Tide]. It was different, but, you know, I think a piece like that [editor – Eruption] has become so engrained, it just sounds different, too different perhaps. Even if it is sonically pleasing, you tend to go back to that feeling of what made it so appealing originally, I don't think it ever gets old.

Greg. I have spoken to some fans that really, really enjoyed the Conquering Tide record, the historical tale and such. It is reassuring that when you do your best, it resonates with some. We just tell ourselves when we look back at releases in the catalog and you realize that we really struck gold during those early years, repeatedly. Maybe if we only had done middling work then and built up to the current record it would perhaps be recognized as a keystone piece, you know. But, you can't change history, and our history has been very kind to us.

Carl. We have the experience now that we don't panic if something doesn't instantly catch on. We have the substantial catalog, we have the consistency. If we had these tremendous gaps between releases and they were weak or kept on getting progressively worse, then we would have to reconsider where we are, or where we want to go.

Keith. So Far to Fall was a bit of a leftover track from around the Fanfare album. We always like to have a fallback in case something doesn't work out, which we learned from The Barbarian on the first album. In this case, we had it in our pocket with Fanfare for the Common Man itself in case Aaron Copland didn't give his approval. That would have been more than slightly unfortunate as we now know! While this was a piano based song originally, I had envisioned this with quite a bit of brass, but we wound up not having to record it. It's a nice, quirky number that was a bit unlike what ELP was known for at the time.

Greg. Although not recorded at the same time, I see some similarity with So Far to Fall and Brain Salad Surgery, the song. Lyrically, they're a bit of an extreme departure from what ELP is known for, for both songs, I can see that. It's always nice as an artist to briefly step outside the box, but I'm not so sure if fans feel the same way. I mean, we obviously don't want to do something that leaves people shaking their head. People follow you because of what you've done, and to stray drastically off that path isn't a good idea.

Carl. With So Far to Fall it shows that we were always looking at ways to evolve the classic ELP sound. We have our acoustic songs, the concept pieces, the classical adaptations. Back then, we also felt we had to be more careful in not going completely off script. But, with those shorter songs that still have the ELP approach of heavily accented rhythms, unpredictable starts and stops, or in my case rhythmically following the theme or the melody, it's something that nobody else really does.

Keith. The acoustic shows were part of a plan that ELP has always had as a sort of plan B when we first formed...if things go wrong on a wider scale, or longer than anticipated, what would we do to survive? We needed something to fall back on, something substantial. We had discussions early on in the band's life that, what if, after the debut or even after Tarkus, things go wrong and we have to cut back on our equipment and investments. We would need a way for the band to recoup our advances and sustain itself within our means. One obvious answer was to do a simple, acoustic presentation of our music, or if not acoustic, at least greatly simplified. As it turns out, it wasn't necessary but was fun to do for the long-time, loyal fans that are aware of the references or the pseudonyms we chose.

Greg. To hear the songs as originally conceived, by Keith or me, or by the three of us, brought back the excitement when these pieces were first created. This is something we've tried to emulate with the incognito shows. We thought, not only would it be quite nice to present these songs acoustically, but to give the audience a feeling what it was like to be with us in the rehearsal hall or studio as these songs first came to life, before the heavy production and instrumental enhancements and expanded arrangements.

Carl. Not only do we have a substantial catalog that continues to grow, but so many of our songs translate to acoustical presentation quite naturally. I'm sure it's because of Greg's many songs and of course Keith with the piano, but also because ELP's songs are unique and thoroughly identifiable regardless of the presentation. We don't need endless, roaring volumes to showcase the songs.

Keith. It's always interesting how an unexpected suggestion takes on a life of its own within the band's sphere. I think, all those years ago, we were worried because we had invested large sums of money in the Moog, a decent PA, and we thought to ourselves...what if things fall apart, for whatever reason, and we have bills to pay?

Greg. Since Keith and I both compose on our respective acoustic instruments, and Carl can play effectively on the smallest or the largest kit, we can really showcase the essence of ELP beyond what wound up on the album, and this is not only the obvious acoustic tunes like Lucky Man and From the Beginning. This really was unexpectedly enjoyable; we might do it once again if we can make it work.

Carl. ELP never was a club or small venue band, so this is almost like purposely going in reverse, by choice and with a clear plan. We're going back to a beginning we never had due to our timing, debut, and good fortune. It was a bit of a surprise at first, even when one's expecting it. When you walk on stage in a small venue and you see a sparse smattering of equipment and you realize you need to make it work, there's no hiding for anyone.

Keith. Not that it will probably matter, but I hope that the acoustic format will

153

prompt some naysayers to at least look beyond the so-called bombast of ELP. We actually already have done so over the years with the restrained performances on Take a Pebble and various piano pieces, but, who knows. I don't want to be negative, and we're certainly not undertaking this approach to satisfy the critics, but we're doing this because it was so warmly received by the hard-core fans.

Greg. I must say that I am quite pleased with the audience reaction and behavior with the acoustic shows. I think the band and the audience have had to recalibrate themselves somewhat because we're all so used to going from a wall of roaring sound, to the roar of the audience, and then on to the next piece with the same result. So when we go from one of Keith's piano pieces to Jeremy Bender to the Fugue from Trilogy and then maybe to Closer to Believing, there is a different ambience that everyone seems to understand; both the artist and the audience.

Carl. Playing more restrained has given us all some insight as to how we can continue to enrich the existing arrangements. Slight changes or accents when done at a reduced level of intensity can sometimes be more startling than at a high volume, because you're already getting pummeled, right? Things can get lost or just overwhelmed by volume, which is why ELP focuses so much on precision, and when all three of us are locked in it sounds both precise but not lost in a soup of multiple guitars and whatever.

Keith. We haven't started discussions on a new record just yet. Touch and Go was positively received, more so than Conquering Tide, yet Touch and Go didn't have a concept piece which the fans always are asking for. I'm not sure how much cross-over effect we had with that record, but it is a bit of a paradox.

Greg. Certainly the lack of a single probably hurt any chance of widespread recognition outside the ELP fan base for Conquering Tide. Touch and Go, at the time, received quite a bit of airplay, which propelled the album quite well in North America, even when Lay Down Your Guns went nowhere as the next single. We are always writing new material, but we'll never write and record because it's the so-called thing to do. If we have something that is up to the ELP standard, we'll

154

tackle it head on.

Carl. We haven't yet revisited the Fanfare and Pirates era where we had a lot of material that was very individually focused. If you look back, we had pieces then that were very distinctly Keith, Greg, or I. Now, we are focusing much more on group efforts. I do miss the eclectic nature of Keith having his piano pieces, Greg and his ballads, and then myself with the drum heavy numbers or classical adaptations in addition to the group pieces. It's just a different mindset for ELP these days, it doesn't mean that we can't or don't want to go back to it. I actually could at a moment's notice and I would enjoy it, but the songs we have produced as of late continue to be very strong.

Chapter Eleven

Black Moon, 1991-1992

Emerson, Lake, and Palmer

The Alternate History

1975-2000

ELP's second incognito acoustic tour lasts through October 1990. After taking a break, the band congregates in October 1991 to write and record a single album with the working title of Unconditional which later was changed to No Surrender. In June 1992, ELP release a single album with the final agreed upon title, Black Moon, and in August they embark on an extensive intercontinental tour. For the first time in their history, ELP traverse Eastern Europe and the former Soviet Union. Paper Blood and Affairs of the Heart are released as singles, neither of which chart.

Black Moon

Track listing

1. Black Moon

(Emerson, Lake, Palmer)

2. Paper Blood

(Emerson, Lake, Palmer)

3. Affairs of the Heart

(Emerson, Lake)

4. Romeo and Juliet

(Sergei Prokofiev; arranged by Emerson)

5. Farewell to Arms

(Emerson, Lake)

6. Changing States

(Emerson)

7. Check it Out

(Emerson, Lake)

8. Creole Dance

(Alberto Ginestera; arranged by Emerson and Palmer)

9. Better Days

(Emerson, Lake)

10. Footprints in the Snow

(Lake)

11. Close to Home

(Emerson)

Keith. I have heard a bit of disappointment that we didn't have a concept piece on the new record, but this is not anything we do consciously anymore. The Touch and Go record had a couple of longer tracks as well, but no concept piece; and I see Black Moon much the same way. I think this is one of the most balanced records we've done even if it is a bit light on the pure progressive side, although I do wish we could have given Carl a bit more of a solo feature.

Greg. The break turned out to be a great rejuvenator and motivator lyrically and to instill some musical spontaneity. You know, it was a nice vacation in Italy, the unfortunate conflict in the Middle East, social observations in daily life. Also, because we rehearsed in Cricklewood in northwest London, I was able to reflect on the challenges and paradoxes one sees daily in a world city. I think that as one's life experiences increase it can't help but be a motivation or a source lyrically as well. Surrealism and fantasy, or science fiction, as lyrical topics always have been strong in so-called progressive music, I enjoyed it going back to my early days in King Crimson. I do think it still has its place in ELP.

Carl. Keith was playing this rather brutish piece of piano music [editor - Creole Dance] during rehearsal several years ago. I thought it was magnificent, I instantly heard a drum pattern as I did for Eruption or, except that I played the drums first in that case. So, I thought it would be nice to just do an orchestral percussion accompaniment with piano, as I did with Atropos from the first album, although that was the whole kit. Not quite the same, but it worked out quite well. We finally got around to recording it properly, and I think we'll do it live also. The record company at first wanted to make it available on the Japanese release only as a bonus track, which we persuaded them not to do.

Keith. We had a brief discussion regarding an outside producer, but while we all are involved in the production of our albums, even going back to our debut, we acknowledge Greg's contributions as the producer. He absolutely has a knack for choosing the right take, the right solo, the patience with the edits, and he obviously has the track record to prove it. He also pointed out, quite nicely, that I already had a song named On My Way Home from the Conquering Tide record, and now I have Close to Home.

Greg. The others know that my production focuses on the band; all you have to do is look at the Memoirs record. I only had one song as compared to Keith's and Carl's side-long pieces. I am always happy to continue to produce when asked, and to assist when asked. The others know that what I do is done for the band, and only with the band in mind.

Carl. This was the first album, well, in quite some time, where we considered doing a few tracks on our own, making all the decisions of the tracks you bring to the table, and then combining forces on the remaining album tracks. We thought that would be a nice way of breaking down the individual, contributing elements of ELP; sort of a throwback to the Fanfare and Pirates era. But, as usually happens, there is such good input that we decide to all work together on tracks best suited for ELP unless it's more palatable as a true solo type track, such as a piano solo, or an acoustically driven piece.

Keith. The record company surprisingly picked Paper Blood as the first single, and it has been relatively positively accepted thus far with airplay in the cities where ELP always has been popular; as far as one would think how far an ELP single would go in today's market. While perhaps not as complex, I hope the fans recognize it in the same vein as The Barbarian and A Time and A Place, with that sort of heavy, driving organ. I don't really know as judging singles to fit in the current marketplace is something I know absolutely nothing about; I leave that up to the record company. I do think Black Moon as a single would have been more reflective of ELP; it's a more ambitious composition, more obviously ELP. Perhaps it was too ELP-like as a single, but again, not my area. It was probably considered too long or too adventurous for radio, and I'm not a fan of hacking up a song to make it nice and radio friendly and neither are Greg and Carl, although we've experienced success that way before. We have put our foot down in the past regarding overtly commercial ventures or representations of the band.

Greg. As management started exploring the tour itinerary, we realized that we would be playing countries where ELP has been well-known and appreciated but,

159

due to political reasons or world events, never had the opportunity to play before. We understand that these fans have an immense emotional attachment to the classic ELP material that was prohibited due to the authoritarian life that existed there in the 1970's and 1980's, and we want to do their expectations justice. For example, all three of us instantly knew that for every show we'll be playing east of the former Iron Curtain we would be playing Pictures at an Exhibition in its entirety at probably every stop, no question.

Carl. Playing places we've never visited before is always quite special. You watch your record sales over the years in certain regions and you're cautiously optimistic that there will be interest once they start advertising the shows. In our case by having an extensive legacy catalog, it could give us an advantage over, say, a newly breaking mid-level act. We have relative confidence that fans of the band that missed out during our first 20 years, or ones that have recently discovered ELP, will seize the opportunity to see us live, and we do not intend to disappoint. I just hope that 20 or so years on, we're not too late for some fans that had followed us since the debut. There is a concern that the infrastructure in some of these places will not be up to the necessary standard that we see in Western Europe, the USA, or Japan to deliver performances at the level we've set.

Keith. I had started playing Creole Dance around 1986, but of course I've been aware of it for a long time. And, I believe it was Carl, of course, [laughs] who suggested that he do a percussion accompaniment, sort of like Toccata from Brain Salad Surgery. Except, he turned that into a drum solo! I mean, my piano pieces are my own, but I've done plenty of piano pieces, and I have plenty more in reserve, so why not? And so, instead of it being a band performance, it worked out quite well using a pure percussion approach, after all the piano is a percussion instrument. I already had agreed to make Changing States a band performance, so, why not have another go.

Greg. The last addition to the record was Check it Out which was actually an extra track from the Conquering Tide recording sessions. Keith brought forward a newer keyboard-based arrangement instead of an acoustic guitar-driven idea I had and along with some arrangement input from Carl, it brought it more in line with the rest of the tracks. Since we already had Footprints in the Snow and Affairs of the Heart as acoustically based tracks, we didn't want to upset the balance of the album. We were initially worried that it might be too close in feel and form to something like Better Days, but it stands on its own; it turned out quite well I think.

Carl. Rehearsals were extremely productive this time around, and I was able to provide significant input on Black Moon and Paper Blood. It wasn't so much in the direct composition but with the arrangements, and Keith and Greg were kind enough to credit me. We've gotten much better with that than we were in the past. Getting credit is nice, but I also realize it's not a personal necessity; I didn't have any writing credits on Brain Salad Surgery which turned out quite well I would say.

Keith. Changing States really reminded me of how Toccata Con Fuoco [editor – from ELP's Pirates album] developed. I had what I thought was this keyboard only composition that changed direction once the band joined in spontaneously while in the studio. Sort of like Fanfare [editor – Fanfare for the Common Man] really, but obviously those pieces have significantly more layers, more distinct sections.

Greg. There continue to be signs of our internal development as a band, even now, more than 10 years on. Keith was immediately receptive and encouraging to Carl and me helping Changing States form and adapt to a band piece. It's something in the past that we would have done as well, but not as easily as we do now. You also run into situations as the years have added on to your career and you find yourself unconsciously revisiting a certain theme or themes, streams of thought. Farewell to Arms certainly has the appearance of the same flavor as Lay Down Your Guns, but of course it's a completely different story.

Carl. Around the Fanfare and Pirates albums, you could see there was a definite trend of the three of us developing very individualistic tracks. There would be input from everyone, but there tended to be not much deviation from the original proposal. I think what I see now is a much more willingness from the composer,

161

any of us, to really take any input and suggestions to heart. As one gets older, one realizes the value of honest and sincere collaboration.

Keith. It was very special playing Pictures at an Exhibition at our few shows in Russia. The response was quite manic, and when we followed up with Romeo and Juliet it really brought down the house. I convinced the others to play it a bit quicker which I think was more in line with Prokofiev's intention. It's less ponderous and there seems to be more tension and unease that way, especially considering the storyline it is supporting.

Greg. We all knew, without a doubt that Pictures [editor – Pictures at an Exhibition] would go down a storm behind the former Iron Curtain. After a couple of shows we had the most unique experience as we talked about how it felt almost the same as when we first played it when our career started out. There was a genuine excitement that we were breaking new ground back then. But playing it here, the excitement is motivated by the reality of hearing music that actually originated there and was outlawed in this new form, but now they get to hear it again; it's quite special. It's as if we're a small part of a greater validation that this is a new world now.

Carl. The shows in the former Soviet-controlled areas were a bit of a shock as far as the standard of living goes and what was passed off as acceptable. Every place we went to the organizers and promoters went out of their way to ensure we could put on a trouble-free, professional show, which we did most of the time. Some of the support functions just were not acceptable, and catering was rather terrible for the most part. But, we soon recognized that many of the promoters really had to pull out all the stops just to make it barely happen. Seeing this dedication ensured we were highly committed as well; it was a bit of a throwback to our early days in that regard. It was all very sincere and memorable.

Keith. ELP doesn't feel threatened by the new genres we've seen as of late, like grunge or hip hop and rap. We've gone through this before when dance-oriented music came to the forefront and then of course the classic clash with punk rock. Every time there's a new fad or fashion we were warned that this is it, it's certainly curtains for ELP now. But it seems that we continue to have a dedicated faction that follows us, and of course there's always an element that is interested in the non-mainstream or non-traditional music that populates our catalog.

Greg. I really don't approach the acoustic guitar by anything other than what the song calls for, the melody, the lyrics; sometimes the mood or the feel. Footprints in the Snow is very close to Lucky Man and Lend Your Love to Me Tonight as they are both have a more simple, straight-forward strumming style...more basic chords one could say. Whereas with From the Beginning, Still You Turn Me On, and I suppose, C'est la Vie and For You, all have less pedestrian, more complex chords, and a lot of cross picking as well. Sometimes an unusual chord provides an anchor for an idea, like the chorus break in From the Beginning, or maybe it's a series of notes within a chord, like I Believe in Father Christmas. A lot of people don't seem to know that The Sage [editor – from ELP live album Pictures at an Exhibition], while using my title, lyrics, and melody, is actually based on a traditional, classical guitar piece called L'Essence.

Carl. I do think Black Moon is an album representative of ELP, but I do miss the epic piece, you know, it's what we're known for. Conquering Tide might not have been very popular, but it is a signature ELP album in my opinion. Touch and Go and Black Moon are very good, but it's missing that crowning touch that the epic pieces provide on our other albums. It falls just a bit short of the ELP standard. But having said that, Black Moon did quite well in Germany [editor – DE #45], so there was something, an element that caused some kind of fan resonance or connection to classic ELP.

Keith. On this tour, we've noticed an interesting phenomenon with the internet becoming more prominent. Our setlists are being shared in advance courtesy of attendees who apparently keep notes and then share it. I mean, I don't mind. I hope that we've chosen the right tunes so that people have something to look forward to. But, it does take away a bit of the magic, you know, it takes away some of the surprise or surprises of the show. I imagine it won't be much longer before the actual audio and maybe even video of a whole show starts being shared on the internet.

Greg. I don't see it as a necessarily negative thing that people know in advance what you'll be playing. It is the way things have become, really. There's always going to be some fan or fans whose favorite tunes we don't play; I think that's a reality of any group that has a substantial catalog, you know? Will some fans not attend knowing we don't play Tarkus or Karn Evil 9 in its entirety? That's very possible, absolutely. Will some fans decide to attend should they see a setlist that excites them? I suppose that's also a possibility, we hope so. I trust the fans understand we do our best, working with our management and gauging the historical and regional interests, to present a broad, historical representation of ELP in a live setting.

Carl. Since a live show is dictated by many aspects, a curfew, the stage presentation, lights, effects, it's difficult to drastically change things. There is room for perhaps an extended improvisation on a piece, but to change the setlist show-to-show or at the drop of a hat; it's not a great likelihood. ELP is known for professional precision in music and presentation; we're not going to change that.

Chapter Twelve

Pax ELP, 1993

Emerson, Lake, and Palmer

The Alternate History

1975-2000

Following the conclusion of the extensive worldwide tour in support of Black Moon in March 1993, ELP release three, triple live CD sets the following August that highlight their international touring career – Pax Europa, Pax Atlantica, and Pax Pacifica. Digging into the archives of over 20 years of recorded ELP concert history, Pax Atlantica is culled from various shows played in North America, Pax Europa from shows in Western and Eastern Europe, while Pax Pacifica does the same from shows played in Japan and the Far East.

Keith. As we fast approach the 25th anniversary of the band, we believed it was time to reflect. There is a huge element of gratitude on our behalf, and to give the fans a real keepsake, something special for all of those that have faithfully followed us and watched us in concert over the years, maybe if they couldn't attend a particular show or tour, or were never able to see us in concert at all. We wanted to give them a true historical record of what ELP as a live band has been like for the past 20-something years. It was a moving experience to hear these live albums played in full, and to bring back all the memories as ELP has evolved.

Greg. It would have been easy just to put all our studio albums into one gigantic bundle and toss it out there or just issue a greatest hits live collection. But, every band does that, right? Since ELP has always been a demonstrable live band, an international band, we wanted to do something a bit more special than just reissue product. By recognizing the live performances we have done around the globe, we came to this conclusion. We have several archivists that have meticulously preserved quality, key recordings that, I believe, are the perfect record of ELP's live performance history from the very beginning. It's a shame we didn't do that more often with film early on.

Carl. The Brain Salad Surgery album and tour was certainly a highpoint in ELP's history, but we decided to use [live album] Welcome Back My Friends 1974 release date as the anniversary benchmark for these live sets. I'm not saying that we will never replicate those heights again, but regardless, it was a time when everything was going our way.

Keith. When we were reviewing the final track listings and deciding what was going to be represented, I did feel a tinge of regret that some key works in ELP's history could not, or as we perhaps felt, should not, be represented. It was a difficult decision since some of these pieces are held dearly by some fans. You know, Memoirs, Carl's percussion concerto, The Enigma [editor – The Endless Enigma]; it is inescapable that some things were very rarely or never performed, or not very well [laughs] and unfortunately had to be left off.

Greg. There were some questions as to why we would have three separate, but almost similar, releases? The truth is that we have noticed there is a marked difference in the western and Far East audiences which has an effect on the aura of the concert and ultimately the performance. Although, to be fair, this difference is less drastic and obvious now than it was in the 1970's. I first noticed the big difference when we played the Tokyo Budokan in I think it was 1983, and MTV [editor – dedicated music video television channel] even gave us a favorable snippet. The band thought it would be appropriate to give the fans a real capsule of what the shows were like for them, to revisit their experiences, or for someone who was never able to attend a show.

Carl. We were considering one triple album, but while the USA was probably the most important regarding ELP's initial overall career impact, Japan has also been such a tremendous part of ELP's career as has Europe which of course, is our home. I mean, for Japan it's not just the sales and the concerts, but for the fans going all the way back to our first visit in 1972. Their loyalty is a unique and very intense one; it is something we dearly treasure. It is something we only see in pockets of the USA and Europe, in college towns or where there is some technical industry. But when it comes to Japan, we see it throughout the country, in elements of society both young and old, spanning generations. For these reasons, we specifically wanted to do the Pax Pacifica release, it's that important to us. And you know, it's not just the fans or the general audiences, there are many in the media in Japan that were and are smitten with ELP; this is for us very, very special. I think the reason it's so special to ELP is that in almost all other parts of the world, there is such an adversarial relationship with much of the press, even though the fans are wonderful. But in Japan, it's as if the entire country has taken us to heart. To see this on a national level is wonderful and very encouraging. We wanted to recognize them and thank them, for their part of the ELP legacy.

Carl. The Japanese are just amazing hyper-specialists of the band in truly all aspects. It's astounding as to their in-depth knowledge, the details within the details, their non-stop inquisitiveness. We get questions about cymbal circumference, or the differences in the type of plectrum Greg used on Tarkus or Trilogy, and let's not even start about the questions Keith gets, they are completely legitimate and unending! Sometimes it feels like they are the band, we just play the music. I predict that in the future there are going to be some amazing ELP tribute performers and acts in Japan from all generations.

Keith. If you look at ELP's history, the first thing we did was play live, and we've always placed a strong emphasis on the live show. It is an undeniable element of what makes ELP, ELP. As such, documenting this was very important. It wasn't easy, especially considering the sheer volume of material available, but it was important enough for us and our organization to make the effort, and to be thorough and do it right.

Greg. We came very close to losing the recording for one of the orchestral shows, in Montreal, an island of Europe in North America as we call it. We were planning to record it and had committed to using one of the first digital multi-track machines and, you know, what we had to do to present the band and orchestra live was quite the undertaking. Thankfully, Michael [editor – Michael Leveillee, ELP live sound engineer] discovered a problem and there was a last minute mad dash to fix it. Thankfully it was corrected literally just before the lights went down.

Carl. We've been fighting the bootleggers since the very beginning of ELP's live performance career; it always was a bother and a distraction. So, rather than fighting them, we just started enlisting them, if you will. I mean, searching the crowd for equipment, impounding it, it was a headache...it was a fine line between encouraging and having them see things our way. It was our secret if you will. I can't tell you all the details, but it was more involved than just a meal and a t-shirt. It allowed us to retain a record of the concert that may not have been the most pristine recording, but we definitely saved some historical performances that otherwise would have been forever lost.

Keith. Well, bootlegs are a sensitive topic for many artists, maybe not so much anymore, but certainly back in the day when distribution was fanatically controlled it was seen as a problem. I think Carl especially had the foresight to see that eventually, many years later, there would be a demand, even with the same tracks as on the official releases. But there is something unique about each concert, you know. Sometimes the raggedness of the recording gives it a bit more energy, rawness, and some nights are just better than others for any number of reasons. I myself haven't given them much of a listen, but I tell you what I find hilarious are the titles. Management gave me a list of some of the better ones here...just a moment. So, here we have, let's see, Bologna's Bolero, thank you for that, then there's Celestial Doggie, The Lobster Quadrille, delightful word salad, and one of my real favorites, 21st Century Schizoid Sheriff. Where are these people when we're looking for an album title?

Greg. We recognized early on that bootlegging could be worked to our advantage. Rather than fight it, we simply made it work for us. I just couldn't see the point in going full-on Peter Grant [editor – Led Zeppelin manager and famous, unrelenting pursuer of their bootlegged material] in the matter, and I couldn't see ELP's audience taking this Grateful Dead approach either. On the other hand, regardless of what an artist or the management does, sometimes matters take on an inertia and life of their own. We're all familiar with Bob Dylan's Great White Wonder Bootleg, even though that wasn't a concert bootleg per se, and then of course there is the infamous Rolling Stones live bootleg [editor – Live'r Than You'll Ever Be]. Bootlegging is just something any artist with any kind of popularity, long or short-lived, has had to contend with.

Carl. Putting the bootleggers out of business is a noble goal, but one is always playing catch-up, and then of course the technology today is light years beyond what it was in the '70's. On the other hand, by being persistent and seeing that the money, however insignificant it may be, makes its way into the right hands, is good enough for me. One has to be tenacious and surrounded by dedicated people in this profession, with both the music and the business side.

Keith. When listening to the material from the early '70's, I'm always a bit shocked at how fast we played pieces, literally all the pieces. I mean, I know we were trying to make a point, and there was a bit of showing off, of course. I think we have now mastered the expressiveness of the pieces so much better. We can still play them fast, and some of them we do, but if everything is played like a whirlwind, you do lose something. Eruption, sure, that demands a fast tempo, Hoedown as well. But certain sections of Pirates we play so much better now, and the same goes for Stones of Years and especially The Great Gates of Kiev, you can take in the majesty of the piece and the lyrics so much better, and it makes the transitions and endings very emphatic.

Greg. I think I listened to our live shows from the vaults for literally a week

169

straight, probably eight hours a day. And while there were few moments as a singer I wish I could take back, I actually found myself absorbed by the different bass tones and approaches I've had over the years. I was a bit worried that, especially with the older material, there would be some wince-worthy moments. But all things considered, I think it mostly fit the material quite well, and of course it was representative of the time, you know, different technologies coming to the forefront, experimentation. Starting out with Fender, you had that classic, warm sound, followed by the Ripper [editor – made by the Gibson guitar company] and that delightful top-end punch it had. Then I had the Alembic eight-string, which could be a clanky at times, but when the sound was dialed in, it was so unique, and it sounded magnificent. The Steinberger played quite nicely, but I didn't like the balance; I thought the Spector from around Touch and Go and Conquering Tide had a nice sound but it fell just a bit short. The Tune bass I acquired around Black Moon is probably the best pure bass I've ever had.

Carl. So many bands seem to take the easy way out as they get older, they play it a bit slower, they simplify the arrangement, leave some of the trickier sections out. I'm pleased that we've generally stuck to the classic material as we've always played it. I think we adjust the tempos and feel quite a bit better now, and of course as time went on Keith was able to layer more sounds. We still have the manic elements we've had from the beginning, but I think over the years as we've played more together, we've gotten even sharper when it comes to precision, unison playing.

Keith. I'm sure there will be the usual complaining from the critics about ELP, as usual, going over the top releasing three, triple CD sets. All I can say is it's what we're known for and what we do. But really, playing live is what ELP is all about. I still recall Greg and me first interacting in a live setting back in San Francisco all those years ago, then of course we had our dramatic introduction to the world at the Isle of Wight, and then we had the California Jam and numerous other shows. While we've had some popular releases, playing live is really the history and identity of ELP, which is why we treat it and the documentation of our playing very seriously.

Greg. When we first established ELP, we all know from the very first interaction between Keith and me, up to the first rehearsal with Carl, that we had something very, very unique when we played together. For that reason, we treated our live playing abilities as a great resource for the band, the greatest resource actually. As a good band able to create quality original music, we are not one alone in the world; but to also be a great live band, we are among a select grouping.

Carl. ELP is, and always will be, primarily a live band, by that I mean is that our best moments are in a live setting. We know our way around the studio, and we can create top level material. But to have the ability in a live setting, dealing with the elements as it were, and not hiding behind a board, to create the excitement and energy that draws people in, that is our greatest asset. And speaking of being known for something, I've been told that ELP were referred to as a group of solicitors on an American television show [editor – Cheers, presented on the NBC television network], so it seems that we are known...for something.

Keith. The question of ELP playing at high volumes was all part of the plan really, even when we were questioned regarding our classical influences, because they said classical music isn't played at deafening volumes. Greg related to me that King Crimson was also accused of playing very loud, at ear bleeding levels some said. But actually, there's a story behind that, a bit of history. So, in the early 1800's, Berlioz [editor – Hector Berlioz, French composer] invented the modern symphonic orchestra by expanding it and adding much, much, more brass whereas before it was primarily strings. He wrote the Requiem Mass, which was commissioned to be performed outdoors. How was this going to be heard, it had to be louder, right? So all of sudden, the orchestra was playing at volumes never heard before. And before long, some people started paying attention, people like Liszt, Wagner, and Bruckner, one of Carl's favorites. They then started to write music using this orchestral format, Bruckner especially a bit later. This is where distortion came from; Bruckner called for low brass to create a mechanical distortion, almost sounding like a distorted organ. The stacking of elements, unison playing, also was heavily Bruckner and this is something ELP also has done from the very beginning.

171

Greg. Volume and rock go hand in hand, even from the very beginning there was always this tendency or desire to hear it louder, more impactful. King Crimson was quite well known for playing loudly and the intensity was probably heightened with our unusual instrumentation which included the saxophone courtesy of Ian [editor – Ian McDonald] as well as the Mellotron. I still have people tell me to this day that our [editor – King Crimson] performance at The Concert for Brian Jones at Hyde Park in London [editor – 1969] was unbelievably loud. ELP continued this tradition, with our use of dynamics it's very effective and with Keith's ability to sustain chords infinitely on the keyboard much longer than a typical rock guitar, it creates a steel wall of sound.

Carl. The difference between ELP and most other bands, especially guitar oriented bands, is that while we certainly play loud and have even used loud production, remember the cannons from the Isle of Wight and then later used on for Pirates but scaled back some, is that at least we have some back and forth. Some subdued moments, some acoustic moments; it's not just non-stop beating people over the head. If you can make people jump up every now and then, that's using volume effectively.

Chapter Thirteen

Veritas, 1994

In September 1993 ELP enter the studio, and in February 1994 release a single album, Veritas. The titular, lengthy conceptual piece is based on the foundation of Keith's arrangement of Bob Dylan's song Man in the Long Black coat suggested by Carl as the basis for an extended piece. For great interest to audiophiles, ELP has recorded the entire album in Dolby Surround Sound. As a result of this (and the ongoing involvement of Dolby), the album was tentatively titled Best Seat in the House, but this was changed just prior to its release when Dolby's involvement was unexpectedly scaled back. Initially, to heighten the profile of the new Surround Sound approach, Dolby and ELP were very close in presenting a dedicated Surround Sound tour where Dolby would create a specially designed, acoustically neutral, portable pavilion for ELP to perform in and the attendant Dolby sound system to be used. This pavilion would have limited seating, probably less than 400 or 500, but the emphasis would purely be on a heightened and consistent sonic presentation utilizing Dolby's Surround Sound format. The idea was to have it set up in one location, the larger urban areas, for a week at a time to control expenses. Unfortunately, as the plans were explored, costs continued to mount and proved to be prohibitive and the idea, for the time being, was shelved. The Veritas tour starts in March 1994, and Dolby does eventually sponsor a limited number of ELP appearances as part of the overall tour in smaller, highly specific venues where their Surround Sound technology can be properly and effectively showcased. Daddy is released as a single, but does not chart.

Veritas

Track listing

1. Veritas

a. Men in the Long Black Coats

(Bob Dylan, Emerson, Palmer)

b. One by One

(Emerson, Lake)

c. Crescent Moon

(Emerson, Lake)

d. Saved, Alone

(Bob Dylan, Emerson, Lake, Palmer)

2. Hand of Truth

(Emerson, Lake)

3. Daddy

(Lake)

4. Hammer It Out

(Emerson)

5. Heart on Ice

(Lake)

6. Gone Too Soon

(Emerson, Lake, Keith Wechsler)

Keith. ELP's adaptations of classical material are well known and a significant element of what we are known for, but I'm afraid that people automatically assume it has to be material from what is the common perception of the classical repertoire from, say, 100, 200, or 300 years ago. I mean, Ginestera and Copland, whose material we've utilized would be considered mid-20th century and I believe Dylan would be as well as he started in, what, I believe 1962 or 1963? So it shouldn't really be a surprise that we're reinterpreting or adapting what people see as more contemporary material for ELP's use. Perhaps it's just different because of Dylan's standing and reputation in popular music. Of course, my own musical history makes it quite clear that I've always considered Dylan a force. Dylan's influence on contemporary music has undeniably been a very strong one, and of course Country Pie and She Belongs to Me were significant parts of my history with The Nice.

Greg. Dylan's Man in the Long Black Coat is a wonderful, moody piece of music, the lyrics are quite evocative. I'm quite thrilled to have penned something in indirect collaboration with a legendary songwriter and wordsmith like Dylan. I'm not sure how else there ever could be a Dylan-Lake writing credit. Of course, I would never compare myself to Dylan as our styles are very different, but at the end of the day, to a certain degree, story-telling is story-telling.

Carl. Well, I'm pleased to say it was my idea that we use the Dylan piece and apply it conceptually to ELP. The original is a wonderful piece, but to use the mood created by Dylan and then have Keith apply a more advanced musical and harmonic approach and expand upon it, I think, gives us the best of both worlds.

175

Keith. Considering that we are a keyboard-driven band, it falls upon me to utilize the Surround Sound effect most effectively. I'm sure there are some interesting drum effects that can be used as well, but, for our material and for the various layers and the different keyboards, whether MIDI or not, all needs to be taken into account to retain the necessary balance. I've heard that some bands have another player off-stage to supplement their sound.   I don't know, to me it's a bit deceptive. I imagine if it's necessary you have no choice, but for ELP, I'm not so sure; I mean, I'm not even a big fan of sequencers.

Greg. It really shouldn't be a surprise that ELP would record and then eventually play live utilizing a new method of presenting recorded or live music, in this case it happened to be Surround Sound. For example, I mean, in the '70's and '80's we toured in quadraphonic and we also had a release or two in quad, so yes, those are fond memories indeed. I suppose it still remains to be seen if Surround Sound takes off on a greater consumer level, and if so, we'll explore continuing to do so. If the consumer side becomes too exclusive, we won't pursue it. It's important to use this type of technology, or any serious advancement in presentation or production, as a way of delivering the music consistently and skillfully and not reduce it down to the occasional gimmick.

Carl. It was unfortunate that the proposed tour plan with Dolby Laboratories didn't work out; it was very, very close to being finalized and for contracts to be signed. But, at the last minute were advised that Dolby, and we certainly don't blame them, was about to do a massive push for a groundbreaking cinematic adaptation of their technology and they had to scale back their ELP commitment. Rather than footing more of the costs than initially proposed, we graciously bowed out. For all the artistic risks we've taken, ELP has also been cautious regarding business matters. That approach has served us well going back to the '70's. While the general music business model is certainly different, being realistic is still the same. Keep your eyes and ear open, and have one hand on your wallet at all times; that's the best advice I ever received when I first started out. Having done the select Dolby shows, it was very eye-opening and gratifying; we appreciate the partnership very much.

Keith. Through it all, the Hammond, Moog, the Yamaha, and all that's followed and is still to come, the piano is still my first priority, for composing, practicing and analyzing a piece of music. Over the years, I've put together what I think is quite a nice collection of solo piano pieces, both for ELP and eventually my own. Obviously these are mostly original, personal reflections, but I also arrange some traditional pieces.

Greg. Heart on Ice is the real, unassuming sleeper of the record in my opinion. Daddy of course, had a bit of a profile due to the subject matter and being based on an actual event. Interestingly, Heart of Ice was the tune we were discussing when we thought an outside, veteran producer would be nice simply to bounce some ideas of off, just to get an independent, fresh take on the material. The first thing he recommended was to change the song from being acoustic guitar driven to a piano-centric ballad. That was all we needed to hear...no, no thank you, run along now.

Carl. I've been asked about the sparseness of my playing on Daddy and several of The Men in the Long Black Coats segments. I'm rightfully known as a busy drummer, and I always will be, but I also know what a song needs; Lucky Man would be a good example I think. There's no need to turn every tune on its head just for the sake of a roaring drum part. I mean, while it's a completely different style of music, imagine if Ringo had done non-stop rolls and fills on In My Life, it would be dreadful.

Keith. Hammer It Out is one of those truly spontaneous, original pieces. I had the rough sketch of it and shared it at rehearsal when Greg mentioned that it reminded him of Gulda [editor – Friedrich Gulda, Austrian pianist and composer] and the piano improvisations I did during the Brain Salad Surgery tour that showed up on the Welcome Back [editor – Welcome Back My Friends to the Show That Never Ends] live album. That motivated me, so I added a bit more of a boogie flavor, so thank you for the inspiration on that Oscar [editor – Oscar Peterson, US jazz pianist] which gave me the middle part; and there you have it.

Greg. I've probably had the most interesting fan turnabout happen with Daddy more than any other song in the ELP catalog. I knew that a song title like that associated with and originating from ELP would raise more than a few eyebrows. I'm sure a few British fans were wondering if we were having a flashback and doing music for the Appleyards or Rag, Tag, and Bobtail [editor – 1950's British children's TV shows]. I'd read a few fan reactions to seeing the pre-release track listing and there would be questions of, Daddy? ELP is doing a song called Daddy? ELP? The band that has song titles such as The Barbarian, Iconoclast, Pirates, Hellburners, or Bitches Crystal, and then there's...this? But once the album and single were released, and the story and meaning from the song made themselves known, the impression changed literally 180 degrees. I'm happy to say it's been nothing but 100% positive and supportive.

Greg. I wouldn't have seen myself writing something as external as Daddy all those years ago. You know, there was Oh My Father, and that was purely internal, but not as an experience. At this stage in our career, I'm realistic to recognize that we don't have the profile to propel this cause the way it really deserves, but being a small part and having helped bring it a bit further; I'm quite pleased. I did find out that there was an interesting connection as far as song titles go. The track on Tarkus that we did as a tip of the hat to our engineer Eddy Offord [editor – Are You Ready Eddy?] was a very close lift to Little Richard's great song The Girl Can't Help It, written by Bobby Troup [editor – US jazz pianist, singer, songwriter, and actor]. Troup actually also wrote a song titled Daddy, which topped the charts [editor – US #1] with Sammy Kaye [editor – US bandleader and songwriter] in the early 1940's I think it was [editor – 1941]. Of course, there's no connection at all as far as the songs' subject matter, but it is rather amusing to see things like that.

Carl. I was very close to bringing in a very percussion-centric track, but as the overall track listing was forming, I thought it would disturb the flow of the album. I did contribute significantly to the Veritas suite, and that was very enjoyable. Keith and Greg were very receptive to the musical approach and literary theme I had in mind, the recording sessions were one of the smoothest we've had yet.

Keith. When we finished up the album, I was quite pleased you know. I thought we had delivered what one could say was another good representation of ELP. The one thing that struck me afterwards was Greg's piece Gone Too Soon which might sound a bit odd. It's not really prototypical ELP, but I realized that it was a positive bit that was needed to offset the heaviness; it's something we're more conscious of now. Men in the Long Black Coats is rather serious, Hand of Truth is heavy, Heart on Ice is a bit melancholy, and of course Daddy is very, very sad. In the past we've had our knockabout songs like The Sheriff or Jeremy Bender and some others like The Gambler, and it struck me that Gone Too Soon is like that. It's not a jokey song, but it lightens the gravity just enough.

Greg. It's important for an album to have some balance and I think we achieved that thanks to Keith's piano piece Hammer It Out and then Gone Too Soon which Keith and I collaborated on with our long-term technical wizard Keith Wechsler. I think I had the very beginnings of the lyric around the time of Yesterday's Hero; it has that same feel, so quite a while ago. When I completed the lyric and started the music, both Keiths added their touches and we had what I thought represented the more positive sounding side of ELP.

Carl. Veritas won't be our all-time best seller and it's not going to set the charts on fire anywhere, but it is a total credit to the consistency of ELP and where we are 13 or 14 years in on our career as recording artists. We're not enlisting an army of outside writers, and we'll continue to do what we are known for and have done best, that being conceptual pieces along with solid songs and the occasional solo feature. We're not watering down our musical character.

Chapter Fourteen

The 25th Anniversary Celebration, 1995

Emerson, Lake, and Palmer

The Alternate History

1975-2000

The ELP Veritas tour, with several small breaks, lasts through October 1994. With 1995 on the horizon, ELP fans had been eagerly speculating and awaiting announcements how the band was planning to celebrate its landmark 25th year since previous landmark year celebrations were somewhat muted. The band lies low through the first half of 1995 when management teased the fans that a significant announcement was forthcoming for ELP to celebrate its silver anniversary. In June 1995, ELP announced that the grand plan to recognize its 25th anniversary was as follows – there was to be no international tour, no album of new material, and no archival album release planned. Instead, ELP has arranged to play three nights at the Royal Albert Hall in London in November with a very unique bill. Opening up for ELP would be The Nice, King Crimson, and The Crazy World of Arthur Brown – with Keith, Greg, and Carl playing with each of their pre-ELP bands – and then followed by ELP proper; each night of ELP would be highlighting different eras of their career. The plan was 25 minutes for each pre-ELP band, followed by two hours of ELP. The concert was promoted as the History and Origins of Emerson, Lake, and Palmer. The response was stronger than expected, upon which promoter Harvey Goldsmith then promptly added two more shows. Amidst the recognition and celebration, there were hints that ELP were planning a gradual move towards retiring but with no timetable set at this time. The night of the second concert, Greg is delayed due to a terrible crash on the M25. King Crimson alumnus John Wetton is in attendance for the concert and offers to perform in Greg's staid, allowing the show to proceed on schedule.

Keith. Well, here we are, hard to believe...25 years of ELP. I remember, you know, being thrilled that we actually got to record Tarkus, which sort of gave us an artistic identity, the identity I was hoping for, and now here we are with our credibility and identity intact, I believe. 25 years is a landmark for anyone as it relates to their profession, let alone with the same company, or the same group of people. Which got me to thinking – how did I get here...with Greg...and Carl. Beyond our individual skills, a huge part of how we were noticed or discovered was due to who we were with before. It was our track record before ELP, what gave us the credentials and our individual profile, if you will, to get the respective attention of the three of us in one form or another, perhaps even prodded on by management. What better way to celebrate than to bring together all the elements that allowed it to happen, that made all of this happen.

Greg. It's been a whirlwind, a sort of days of years, and plenty of hard work in between. We had some ideas as how best to commemorate it, you know? Of course, there was the obvious; a big show, obviously in London, a big release of...something, greatest hits, whatever. But, that's been done to death, right? Then, I believe it was Keith, who had the idea of creating a show of the history of ELP, a pre-ELP show as part of an ELP concert. Not just a mammoth anniversary ELP show, but a show including the bands that we all were members of before, a truly once-in-a-career event. Of course, coming up with the idea is one thing, executing it with all the different people, personalities, schedules, management, that's the real work there [laughs]. This is exactly why we always have Stewart [editor – Stewart Young, ELP manager] at an arm's length.

Carl. When Keith first brought this up, I thought it was fabulous as did Greg. And I have to tell you, to get all three of us to instantly agree on something, it's a rarity;

so we figured we had something very, very good, a magnificent event for ELP and the fans. And considering that most of the major players are still with us, God bless them; what timing. What an opportunity to take advantage and create an event of this significance, lasting personal significance, and for the fans.

Keith. We had heard from management that there is quite the internet presence of ELP thanks to some very, very devout fans. Obviously we have our own web sites, but there are more than a number of fan-based ones as well. Just one to mention, there's a wonderful digest that keeps tabs on ELP activity and scours the news for bits and pieces of all things ELP. Let me see here, there's ELP being mentioned on TV quiz shows, the various bootlegs floating around, the ones Carl hasn't snapped up [laughs], and even how best to play the left hand on Eruption, Manticore, or Infinite Space. I read it, and it even got me thinking about how I play it; it's wonderful, really.

Greg. The World Wide Web is going to be dominant in all facets of our lives; we haven't even begun to scratch the surface regarding its commercial or business potential. I'm certain there are business mavericks and moguls contemplating this right now. As computers become more powerful and affordable, I believe remote musical collaboration will become routine as it will no longer be constrained by distance, even for those where music is not a profession, but a hobby. I was quite surprised when management pointed out the number of ELP fan sites; the level of detail regarding our various histories that they have recorded is amazing. I've actually forgotten some of the things they've saved in the forms of interviews and old print media clippings. Our management is going to have to do better!

Carl. I think what most people miss out on with the web is that it will become a societal accelerator, as everything will be made easier and quicker, and for more people, not just those in positions of means, power, or influence. I'm already thinking about what more powerful computers and faster communication can do in the form of organizational communication, business, and sharing large pieces of data, whether it's business, music, or art. So much time is wasted on administration and sharing information, meetings, endless reviewing, getting

182

approval, all that stuff; this will change that, hopefully.

Keith. I must admit I was a bit worried how the lads from The Nice would react, or feel about this, after all, it was me leaving that effectively broke up the band. [Pauses] I know there was some talk about the financial disasters that Immediate Records had as being the problem, but I have to be honest of course. I do think, well I know for sure, that The Nice contributed so much not just to my career, but to establishing progressive rock. It was a great relief to me, for them, after ELP got some momentum that Elegy [editor – The Nice's final official album release, 1971] was rather successful [editor – UK #5]. I was so thrilled that they accepted to do this; there is a true feeling of eternal camaraderie. I can, but I can't explain it.

Greg. That Bob [editor – Robert Fripp, guitarist and leader of King Crimson] agreed to do this in the midst of his commitments to King Crimson speaks volumes of our relationship going back more than 30 years. We spoke privately, at length, and quite warmly, and I'll keep those details private. After speaking with Bob, I recalled that all of us that were part of the beginnings of the so-called progressive movement found ourselves in London and the whole hippie counterculture movement; call it the Cultural Revolution if you want. But at the end of the day, I think that the members of ELP and these other groups, we couldn't help but be British and that the idea that we had to be part of the greater counterculture just didn't resonate. Of course, I'm speaking artistically or musically, not necessarily in morals or habits. I mean, we were, and still are, accused of being sellouts. But, we really would have been sellouts if we had just jumped on the bandwagon with the rest of the shirts and gone totally against the path we had already started to forge. It was an unforgettable time.

Carl. The amount of goodwill that came out of this experience I will forever treasure. I mean, I hadn't met some of the guys in The Nice or [King] Crimson before, or perhaps very briefly many years ago. But in speaking with them, I see bits of Keith and Greg in most of them musically and in some of them personally, and vice versa.

Keith. When the ELP fan club wanted to have a convention, while we couldn't personally attend we thought it would be nice to do something special for the attendees; these obviously very, very dedicated fans of ELP. We had an orchestral version of Abaddon's Bolero in the vaults; it was something we did when we were seriously considering elevating the orchestral presence with the band, but anyway. It was being saved by the record company for some kind of rarities release, an anniversary compilation, or something. But we convinced management to just play it at the convention. It'll eventually get a proper release of course, but why not allow the diehards to have an early peak at something? I thought it was a nice thing to do, we all did.

Greg. I'm glad management allowed us to do this. It [editor – Abaddon's Bolero, orchestral version] was never released as such, so we wanted to play it for the fans, these special fans. No one checked for a pocket recorder or anything, there was no need, and that would have been inappropriate. This was a preview, if you will, for people who, in our mind, very well deserved this small gesture on our behalf. Once the anniversary shows were even tentatively scheduled, we just had no time. Every day had become just a mad dash so properly attending the ELP fan convention in person and doing it justice wasn't a possibility unfortunately. I mean, what would people think if we just left the car running, dash inside and say hello and be on our way? I would call that insulting, so no. But we certainly are, once again, taken aback by the dedication of our fans. We thought that giving them a sneak preview to an unreleased piece, not just a throwaway track, was at least an authentic acknowledgement from us. I hope it was received as genuinely considerate and respectful as it was intended.

Carl. The initial idea proposed by management was that the each one of us would just do a video greeting for the convention, which we did, but we wanted to do something a bit more. I mean, to recognize 25 years, I think the band certainly could do a little bit extra. My understanding is that some of these fans have been loyally following the band from the debut, so putting forth a little bit of effort on our end even if we were a bit busy, we can certainly do that. And yes, of course, the actual release of the orchestral Bolero will absolutely happen sometime in the future.

184

Keith. There was a bit of a question as to, well, do we select the band that we played in before ELP, or perhaps another one, a more successful one, or our first one or a favorite one? I mean, I had varying bits of success and some popularity prior to The Nice, and Greg had several bands he was in prior to [King] Crimson as well as a few records, and of course Carl had great success with Arthur Brown. But we concluded that we each should look at our histories as moments and accomplishments and choose the one band in our time, that was necessary to build up our reputation just before we established ELP.

Greg. For me, there really was no doubt who I would select. All the bands I played with before ELP were instrumental in my musical journey and maturation, but with the creation and establishing of King Crimson, it was that capstone I had been aiming for. The talent, the professionalism, the songs, the debut, the sheer explosion of popularity, all had indescribable impact. I'm not speaking badly of The Gods or The Shame, but at that time King Crimson was more than just a revelation for those of us in the band, and apparently many others as well.

Carl. Even starting at a young age, I was fortunate enough to have had extensive exposure to high levels of talent and dedication. Whether it was via instruction like Tommy Cunliffe or Bruce Gaylor, or in performance with Chris Farlowe with Albert Lee, then starting with The Thunderbirds, and of course experiencing massive success with Arthur Brown which was just difficult to process; the oddness of it all. Of course, the pinnacle of instruction was with the legendary James Blades [editor – renowned English percussionist] who also tutored the wonderful Evelyn Glennie [editor – legendary Scottish percussionist]. It would have been a big question if I would have chosen Atomic Rooster or Arthur Brown if Vincent [editor – Vincent Crane, Atomic Rooster keyboardist] was still with us since that was my true pre-ELP band which I felt was really happening and really going somewhere, which it was, until ELP came along.

Keith. I really wasn't familiar with John [editor – John Wetton, bassist and vocalist], but when I heard he was in Mogul Thrash [editor – UK progressive rock band] I knew that one of my personal favorite Hammond players, Brian Auger, produced their first album. I don't think he played on that album, which is a shame. But, as you've probably seen on more than one occasion, there's quite a bit of nepotism when it comes to UK progressive bands but for some very simple reasons, being a great player, writer, and performer.

Greg. We had a bit of a scare on the second 25th anniversary night when I was stuck in nightmarish traffic due to a terrible crash on the M25. Since it's such a long show we just couldn't start late and throw the entire production and everything off. Thankfully, Johnny Wetton – who I've known and have been friends with for many years and is a very talented Dorset boy – was part of the King Crimson entourage and it was really just dropped into his lap before show time: would he be willing to step in for me and do the Crimson set? Of course, he's familiar with the material as he was in the band, but still, it's quite an undertaking even with the abbreviated setlist. He graciously stepped in and as expected, did a great job; he's a wonderful singer and a great player. The crowd, many of whom attended multiple nights, got to see a bit of additional history.

Carl. I knew John [editor – John Wetton, bassist and vocalist] was a talent not just from his time in King Crimson, but also Mogul Thrash and Uriah Heep [editor – UK rock band] just to name a few others. If you wouldn't know any better, he and Greg's vocals are quite similar, very similar actually. We had a teleprompter ready for him if he asked for it; it's uncanny how this all unfolded and was resolved.

Chapter Fifteen

The Velvet Coats of Kings, 1996

The Ending Announced

Emerson, Lake, and Palmer

The Alternate History

1975-2000

In May 1996 ELP release – quite predictably – the legendary 1995 History of ELP concerts titled The Velvet Coats of Kings. The band wanted the release to be a true historical record and to cover the different ELP set lists of all three nights. This, of course, resulted in a quadruple album, something which the critics predictably swooped down upon instantly and mercilessly but which delighted the fans even more. With the addition of three more bands, the release's profile was even higher with fans of progressive rock beyond just ELP. Putting to bed the rumors of an approaching end of the road for ELP, the band announces they have selected the year 2000 as their final one for ELP. There will be no tour for 1996 and 1997, as the focus is on a final album for ELP, a concept album to officially seal the band's history with a target release date in 1998. Various tours will then follow up to the millennium; ELP enters the studio in November 1996.

The Velvet Coats of Kings

Album 1 – Night 1

The Nice – King Crimson – The Crazy World of Arthur Brown

ELP

Album 2 – Night 2

The Nice – King Crimson with John Wetton – The Crazy World of Arthur Brown

ELP

Album 3 – Night 3

The Nice – King Crimson – The Crazy World of Arthur Brown

ELP

Keith.   The anniversary concerts will very likely be the highlight of my career...more so than our debut, all the shows in-between and very possibly our last show and album, however that will play out.   That probably sounds a bit strange or maybe even premature, especially so soon after the event, but that is my genuine feeling.   It was as if I was replaying the formative years of my musical life and of Greg and Carl as well, it was truly uncanny.   When Brian [editor – Brian Davidson, drummer for The Nice] started with the cymbals on Karelia, I looked at our friends and family in the wings and everyone had tears in their eyes.

Greg.   When we all played with our pre-ELP bands, it felt like I was watching a movie, a movie that condensed years, the most mentally consuming time one can imagine.   Every detail I can remember, from Crimson to what I can recall of The Nice and Atomic Rooster and recognizing Keith's and Carl's contributions and then hearing those elements in ELP's music, it brought about a flood of memories; an emotional and rational justification if you will.

Carl. It's very rare that I am less than 100% focused on the task at hand, but when I saw Keith on stage, and Greg, and then I was on myself, and then the three of us. It was really almost too much to take in, somewhat overwhelming. I heard more than one person say they wanted it to last a bit longer and savor it.

Keith. Where to start, except to look back how and where it started. I recall saying many, many years ago that the typical lifespan of a band is three years, maybe five if everything lines up perfectly. That was youth speaking and probably a lot of impatience as well. And now, now we're looking at 30 years to naturally seal the history of ELP. We intend on giving this our absolute all, combining all our knowledge and skills and experiences realizing this will be absolutely the band's final, documented statement.

Greg. Shortly after performing the 25th anniversary concerts, we had the most intense, heart-to-heart discussions we've ever had...from the post Welcome Back My Friends era, to Yesterday's Hero and beyond, nothing can compare to the emotions from having been in each other's musical pockets for that long, 30 rather stunning years. It was as if we all understood that it was the most natural thing to do with no bitterness, and no sadness. We now see the end approaching, and it's not an unsatisfying one. Not unexpectedly, for our final work we have decided on putting the emphasis on how ELP has made its mark, with wide-ranging and sweeping epics that have taken the listeners on a journey. And now here we are as the journey is coming to end as we prepare to go 'round one more time.

Carl. The three of us are on such a similar level; this was the most natural discussion one could imagine. There really was absolutely no spite or resentment, none. Having this kind of discussion now would have seemed impossible early on in ELP's career. We have worked incredibly hard, surrounded ourselves with very capable people, and we have been exceptionally lucky. We are determined to bring this to an authoritative conclusion.

Keith. It was a deeply, deeply personal decision, all those years ago, to leave The Nice. You know, The Nice was very much loved by the fans, even by some critics

189

that wound up despising ELP...yeah, it's true, sadly. I think many people, not just critics, have forgotten how important The Nice was to the fusing of styles early on in the progressive movement. But, when I see the type of fan loyalty that ELP has cultivated and the impact and influence we've had, I feel a great sense of justification and also relief that the difficult choice I made was the right thing to do.

Greg. I understand that even after so many years of ELP, that there are still some fans of The Nice, King Crimson, and Atomic Rooster that feel badly that those bands came to an end...and, I understand that, I really do. I absolutely remember when the original Shadows disbanded in 1968, I felt a bit distraught; it's as if there's a hole in one's musical soul. Strangely, some observers of the progressive music scene seemed to think that the album title Velvet Coats of King was a slight at our former bands, because the full lyric line is, 'Exchange your rags, for the velvet coats of kings.' I mean, ELP just aren't that mean-spirited; it was a grandiose lyric which, we hoped, reflected upon the regality of those landmark concerts. We wouldn't speak so cruelly and spitefully of former bandmates and, mostly, friends or the friends of our friends.

Carl. Despite the genuine warmth of the 25th anniversary concerts, I feel a tremendous sadness about Vincent [editor – Vincent Crane, b.1943 -- d.1989, organist and composer for Atomic Rooster] and for his family. I saw what he went through, and how hard he worked to get over his challenge. And he then did, resoundingly, and not just with Atomic Rooster, but with his multitude of collaborations. As a talented composer and player, it was through sheer force of will that he persevered as long as he did. I don't think many people realize that not only was he the co-writer of the international hit Fire [editor – UK #1 in 1968] with the Crazy World of Arthur Brown, but he also wrote Tomorrow Night that did quite well on the charts for Atomic Rooster [editor – UK #11 in 1970]. I dearly wish he was still with us.

Keith. I've been asked many times how we knew to make a decision so far in advance, but when you're in the midst of it all, you know. This isn't a decision that we arrived at just this year. At various times throughout our career, both good and bad, we asked ourselves, how much longer can we make this last? And we took everything into consideration, not just the creative aspect, but our personal lives as well. Regardless of what anyone might say, 30 years is quite a phenomenal run in any business.

Greg. The prospect of ending ELP had come up numerous times, not necessarily at bad junctures, but just through the regular course of time. Sometimes even after finishing an album or a tour that went well, we would ask ourselves, are we up for this again? I'm proud to say we said yes more often than anything else. The 25th anniversary shows, to me, were a big indicator that we should start planning to bow out as gracefully as possible. Not that we were out of ideas, but it just felt like a very natural thing to start discussing, and we all agreed. We didn't want to just simply announce our retirement, play a few shows, and turn out the lights. We wanted to have a clear map, and share our intentions with the fans and those within the organization with plenty of advance notice.

Carl. When time marches on, you come to a point where you realize you have much more time behind you then ahead of you. For ELP, there was no creative deficit, we simply agreed that we have given enough of ourselves as individuals and a band, and the machine had to start winding down. When we agreed to the millennium as the ending, we weighed our decisions very, very carefully. We even challenged each other, you know? I remember asking Keith and Greg, if we choose to bring this to an end – and we all know it's very easy to say yes to something that's four years down the road, sort of like scheduling a difficult doctor's or dentist's appointment – but how about the year before, or when the final year has arrived? How about when we go on stage as a band for the final time? Put yourself in that position, can you then stand by your decision? There was no hesitation from any of us.

Keith. Four years as a 10 year-old is an eternity, as a 20 year-old you realize that it will pass eventually, as a 30 or 40 year-old you'll say that will arrive soon enough, as a 50 year-old you say, I'd like those four years back. There is a great relief knowing when you have set a deadline voluntarily, because – hopefully – you have taken everything into account before agreeing to it. It's both comforting and encouraging that we have a goal, and a very generous timetable for everything to be neatly done.

Greg. I'm sure some are saying that we are taking the route of a typical OAP [editor – old age pensioner] and taking a ridiculous amount of time for our finale. To that I say, yes, we are taking our time, and have earned the right to do so. We're not just three wee lads anymore, we're taking our time because we can, but we're not going to default on our responsibility. ELP will deliver.

Carl. We've been around each other long enough to know when someone is not on the same page, and just the same, we know when we all are on the same page. There is just a wonderful sense of camaraderie now as there's ever been.

Keith. We've discussed the need not to overthink or overdo it. This will be a project just like any other, with the only difference being that it will be our last one. Is it possible to get that out of one's mind? Probably not, it's too paramount of an issue, and I imagine it would be unusual if we did manage to completely ignore that. The main thing to do is to not consciously use the approach of 'we'll never get to do this again, so we better do it now'. If the works flows naturally, like it has in the past, it will turn out best.

Greg. We have always worked well under pressure, whether that pressure is artistic or if its timeline related. For the debut we felt the need to exceed expectations, with Brain Salad Surgery, we needed to shift our emphasis to ensure we could translate the studio product into a live setting, with Touch and Go we need to reaffirm our position as ELP, and those are just a few obvious examples. This is also pressure, but a different type of pressure. It's of our choosing, both the timeline and the finality of the working relationship. So it truly is unlike anything we've experienced, but well with our capabilities.

Carl. Keith summed it all up best, let's not overanalyze every single step of the way. We don't have to worry about producing a quality product; we've learned how to do that. We're not going to end this the way we want with non-stop guesswork and doubting ourselves. We're going to go to work as we've done numerous times before. The only difference is this will truly be the last time.

Chapter Sixteen

Unnecessary Impressions, 1997

Emerson, Lake, and Palmer

The Alternate History

1975-2000

For all of 1997 ELP remain off the road and firmly in writing and rehearsal mode and were frequently ensconced in the studio. The band made it clear that they were totally devoted to their final album which, in a promised nod to their heritage, would be conceptual in scope and, unlike all their previous concept albums, would take up the entire release; there were to be no stand-alone songs. Unexpectedly, the record company did issue a grab bag of outtakes and previously unreleased material in August titled Essential Impressions, which did not sit well with most of the band as it seemed to distract from the heavy focus on the band's final project.

Essential Impressions: Past and Present

Track listing

1. Abaddon's Bolero (Orchestral)

(Emerson)

2. A Blade of Grass

(Emerson)

3. The Pancha Suite

(Palmer, Ron Aspery, Colin Hodgkinson)

4. Preacher's Blues (Live)

(Emerson, Lake, Palmer)

5. Lucky Man (Live – Atlantic Records 40th Anniversary)

(Lake)

6. Fanfare for the Common Man (Live – Atlantic Records 40th Anniversary)

(Aaron Copland; arranged by Emerson)

7. Ocean's Call

(Emerson)

8. Beorma

(Palmer, Andrzej Panufnik)

9. The Last Goodbye

(Mark Mancina)

10. At the Sign of the Swinging Cymbal

(Brian Fahey)

Keith. I had this piece of music, somewhat experimental music if you will, that was a commission for the MSN Rifff platform which was to be some sort of on-line, interactive or participatory program allowing other users, subscribers I imagine, to modify or change it up. The piece, Ocean's Call, was ultimately not used by MSN, and I thought it deserved the ELP treatment. The piece was originally titled Boney Vegetables, and when we met in the studio after the Veritas tour I presented the music to Greg and Carl. They were quite pleased with it and supportive, but then came the title and they both gave me the look, as we call it in ELP. As in, when you make a suggestion and the others give you the look, it means you might want to reconsider or at least rethink what you just proposed [laughs].

Greg. When I heard of the plans to release this album, these tracks, I made it a point that any contribution from my vaults for this shambles of a collection was not going to happen. The record company knew very well what our long-term plans and goals were shortly after the Veritas record. This could have been planned and timed much, much better...just hogwash really, it's not as if we were in the dog box, you know? Also, Preacher's Blues is really not...I mean, it shouldn't even be considered a proper ELP song. It's just a 12-bar ramble that eventually turned into a relatively proper song, that being of course Tiger in a Spotlight, but at the time it was a dabble. Again, this collection of tracks was not acceptable for a release, and certainly done with terrible timing and no foresight or consideration.

Carl. Well, the release of this collection of somewhat rare tracks is a bit of a mystery as far as what we were expecting. I'm hesitant to complain because we have been treated exceptionally well by the record company over the years, but, one has to wonder. I could see this as some type of legacy release after we call it a day, but in the midst of being sequestered away working on the new album that is going to put a bow on our recording career, I just don't know, I don't see the logic at all. I'm happy that the fans get the chance to hear the orchestral Bolero that caught everyone's attention at the fan convention a few years back, as the word had spread, you know. There are a few interesting tracks of historical note for ELP fans, but that's all.

Keith. I've heard Greg's concerns, and Carl's concerns, about the last album, and I certainly appreciate their good business sense, a sort of awareness of the band's arc. But, at the risk of sounding a bit disinterested, that's not me so much; for me it's the music. I know that ELP has developed a very refined approach which appeals to our fans, what some would call professional decorum and integrity, we're not a very drop-of-the-hat kind of band which this release feels like. I do feel that the Bolero was very worthy of a release as was Carl's extended piece Beorma; the rest is a bit what one maybe could call filler. But, there truly are some nice moments, and a bit of spontaneity as well.

Greg. Had the record company thought this through just slightly, this could have been a great release in, say, 2002 or maybe 2003. It would have reflected much better timing regarding the ELP timeline. This could have been a true, from the vaults type collection with the Bolero and Carl's piece as the cornerstones and then flesh it out.

Carl. Around 1975 and 1976 I worked with an amazing Polish composer, Andrzej Panufnik and we collaborated on an extended piece, a ballet, honestly. It was very conceptual and I wanted it to be reflective of my personal history as a native of Birmingham, hence the title which refers to the tribe of people that settled the area probably in the 8th century or so. As ballets go, it probably would be classified as neoclassical, and as one would expect it is more percussion heavy than what one hears in a traditional ballet...but it was enjoyable working with a man like Panufnik who seemed to enjoy the jarring and complex sequences I came up with. Keith also gave some tips and pointers. I'm not sure if it qualifies as an ELP piece, so...but yeah [pause] this release again.

Keith. If this was the early 1970's, then the label probably could have done something with the [Essential] Impressions album that was done quite regularly back then, which was releasing it as a budget album; not treating it like a full-blown, brand-new release if you will. But, considering how the business model has changed so drastically, that wouldn't be considered.

Greg. I will say this, I only would have given this release my support if they would've treated it more like a true legacy release. Remember, when Pictures [editor – ELP live album, Pictures at an Exhibition] was released, it was done so as

197

part of Island Records' budget line. I believe there was a King Crimson album at the time [editor – Earthbound] that got the same treatment, as did the first live albums from Genesis.

Carl. As we approach our grand finale, this release would've been a nice accompaniment to a legacy package, greatest hits you know, a singles collection, something that you know is an inevitable release. So what you would do then, have a typical greatest hits live release remastered, but then using this as an added bonus. I imagine if they wanted to really draw it out, they could've taken a track or two and released them piecemeal with each subsequent greatest hits variant that we know will eventually be populating the ELP catalog.

Keith. As the primary composer, I'm very aware that what we're working on now will be how ELP is viewed historically, whether we like it or not. It seems to have become the default way of looking at a legacy artist; whatever they did last, it doesn't seem to go away for at least 10 years. I'm being true to our past, but also looking forward as we've always done. There will be no obvious references as in with The Score [editor – opening track from ELP's Touch and Go album]. This will be completely new and original, and standing on its unique merits.

Greg. Keith is writing some amazing music, grand in scope and I believe truly some of his best ever, and we also have a concept that I believe you could easily say is international in its appeal. Whereas in the past we have referenced certain social or political matters, and of course some historical fiction as well as true history, this is something everyone can relate to. In a way, I see it as an abstract but direct connection with Tarkus and the principle of laying bare man's inhumanity to man, that's really all I can say right now.

Carl. Yes, we are taking our time, but not because there is a shortage of material or ideas. We have the professional leeway and the advantage of experience as well as great enthusiasm as we work on what will be ELP's final contribution to its own catalog as well as the larger, historical canon of progressive rock. Greg has hinted that the lyrics are related to the deeper meanings behind Tarkus, which is actually quite nice as I've always felt that Tarkus while not our first album, it was

198

our first album as a true, collaborative band as far as writing, composing, and arranging.

Keith. It is very flattering when one looks back at your catalog and you hear that other artists, popular or not, have covered your material. I mean, it's even nice when a pub band does so. I've heard our material a few times while having a drink, and more than a few of them were pretty good! Obviously, Greg's compositions have been covered numerous times, and that's always very nice, nice for Greg but nice for all of us really. I have heard over the years that some of our music also lends itself to special occasions, high profile occasions, and major sporting events as well. I understand that Fanfare [editor – Fanfare for the Common Man] always got a quick nod in the UK and the US, Welcome Back [editor – Karn Evil 9, First Impression, Part Two] is still used regularly in the US apparently for sporting events as was Nutrocker back in the day, and even Black Moon has popped up a few times this way.

Greg. It is, of course, very complimentary when another artist does an interpretation or cover version of your music, you hope it is done in a respectful way of course, just as we've always done with our adaptations of other people's material. [I Believe in] Father Christmas of course has had this treatment several times, but my personal favorite has to be the version of C'est la Vie by Johnny Hallyday [editor – French singer and actor], who is known as the French Elvis. I believe it went top-10 in France [editor – FR #5]. Strangely enough, an American hard rock band called Dokken, I think, did a very nice version of From the Beginning, which is not a hard rock song at all of course, but it was very well done I thought.

Carl. No, no hard feelings at all about Greg's songs getting the cover treatment, he is that kind of writer and is able to generate that kind of appeal. And of course as a singer, it's to be reasonably expected that his tunes would get that kind of recognition. As Keith and I have said on numerous occasions, they are simply great songs. I present myself as a drummer and an arranger, or collaborator, and as a composer my songs are more specialist if you like, and I quite like that.

Keith. The Last Goodbye, from what I recall, was a song from a fellow named Mark Mancina. He was briefly considered as a producer for the Black Moon album as he is very talented and highly regarded, and this was a song he submitted to us, a sort of introduction; an audition of sorts perhaps. As it turned out he instead went on, as everyone knows now, to great success in cinema, which was no surprise really. The song never went beyond the demo stage, but it really shows the potential and an ELP influence.

Greg. Mark [editor – Mark Mancina] was a real find, but real talents tend to get immediately picked up by the highest bidder to which I say, good for him. Would it have worked having an outside producer? Perhaps, as one should never say never; but it's important to recognize that Mark also had a very talented engineer [editor – Steve Kempster]; they would be a most formidable team. Submitting a song to ELP is not for the faint of heart, but he obviously had the talent and the confidence to do so.

Carl. The song Mark Mancina submitted to us, I thought was an interesting blend of prog-like sensibilities with a great regard for the past, but with today's mindset. It is one of those four or five minute songs that you could easily hear being a seven or eight minute song in the '70's. Genesis is very good at that sort of thing, but would it have worked for ELP? I don't see why not, it fits in with our material as far back as Yesterday's Hero or Touch and Go. Mark had been, for some time, a great fan of the band, which is always nice to hear.

Keith. The Brass Incorporated piece [editor – At the Sign of the Swinging Cymbal] was literally just a blast through it because of our relationship with legendary British DJ Alan Freeman; it was his theme song for Pick of the Pops [editor – BBC radio program showcasing the top-20 UK singles; debuted in 1955]. He always spoke well of us. I'm actually shocked that someone found it necessary to record our version, all one minute of it, let alone put it on a compilation!

Greg. Alan Freeman, also known as Fluff, was the top DJ on [BBC] Radio 1 who was a great friend and supporter of ELP; a kind, wonderful man and a lover of music of all types. He was most certainly a loyal ally of ours and a promoter behind the scenes back then. It was interesting to hear us playing his theme song all those years ago, which I actually had forgotten about, although I certainly hadn't forgotten Alan. I'm glad that he was able to do our 25th anniversary show introductions at the Royal Albert Hall.

Carl.   I recall us quickly putting this [editor – At the Sign of the Swinging Cymbal] together as a nod to Fluff Freeman, who is such a friendly and positive guy. I remember Keith coming up with the arrangement and it was great fun. When we did The Man With the Golden Arm theme for the Memoirs tour some years earlier we all actually recalled doing this, that same kind of great, energetic, big band feel.

Chapter Seventeen

Crossing the Rubicon, 1998

Looking Back

Emerson, Lake, and Palmer

The Alternate History

1975-2000

In June 1998, the band declares that timeline and logistical decisions regarding their final original release have been set and an official announcement is forthcoming. ELP reveal on August 19 (the anniversary release date of their 1974 triple live album Welcome Back My Friends to the Show That Never Ends), that their final release of original material, a single album titled Crossing the Rubicon, will be released on November 20, 1998, the 28th anniversary of their eponymous debut, Emerson, Lake, and Palmer. The single album is classic ELP with the title as an extended conceptual piece covering the entire album with no stand-alone songs. ELP have called upon William Neil [editor – UK artist and painter; producer of the cover designs for ELP's albums Pictures at an Exhibition and Tarkus] for the album's artwork. As Greg had hinted in interviews prior to the release, the theme of the album revolves around the concept, and dangers, of human cloning. ELP also announce that the Crossing the Rubicon tour will start in December and is expected to last through April 1999. ELP also provide their tentative final plans, which details that their final, farewell concert tour will start sometime in mid-2000 and culminate in ELP's grand finale in London in November of that same year.

Crossing the Rubicon

Track listing

1. Betrayed

(Emerson)

2. First Breath

(Emerson, Lake)

3. Tyrant of Reason

(Emerson, Lake)

4. Superstition Dawn

(Emerson, Lake, Palmer)

5. Revelation

(Emerson, Lake, Palmer)

Keith. As I started writing the music for [Crossing the] Rubicon, I literally pulled out all the stops I could to make this the most fitting, original statement as we close the door on ELP. I wanted it to have the true seal of approval and deliver what our fans expected for the final expression of ELP, something as fitting and dramatic as we had ever done.

Greg. When I shared with Keith that I'd like to write about human cloning and all of the attendant dangers and pitfalls, I think we both realized that if we commit to this, not just the album and the anniversary, but with the subject matter that it could be nothing less solemn or dignified than we've ever done. I mean, I see it as a natural conclusion to Knife Edge, Tarkus, and Karn Evil 9 where I hinted about man's heartlessness and cruelty to himself, isolation, and technology out of control. Would cloning be the ultimate act to not rid society of undesirables or illness or disease, by preventing it? But who makes these decisions regarding what traits will be allowed or approved, and then what traits to what degree? Who chooses in whose image or example when we will attain a so-called perfect human status? Will our unique human characteristics disappear, even the bad ones, in our attempt to make us perfect? Once the decision is made to clone, the cat is out of the bag, and society will have to cross the Rubicon.

Carl. We have some incredible music and Greg has some lyrics that are as earnest and severe as he's ever done. I think we've timed Rubicon in relation to our planned farewell as best as possible in that we want to tour into 1999 in support of the new album, which will then allow us to focus on a career-spanning setlist for the millennium, anniversary tour, and a suitable grand finale.

Keith. No doubt that Crossing the Rubicon hearkens back to our earlier albums with the darker imagery, that ominous sense. We started that with the debut, continued it with Tarkus, tapered off with Trilogy, but then probably reached its peak with Brain Salad Surgery. Since then we've focused on different themes, but we felt a natural pulling to go back to that direction as a final statement.

Greg. Keith and I both brought forth a presentation style that would be heavy, almost gothic. We had experienced those possibilities, and witnessed the success, in our previous bands that communicating musically with the beauty of classical music styling combined with the human feelings of spiritual desolation, finding oneself in a mysterious world, combined with the energy and potency of rock music would be very powerful. We started that vision, that odyssey, with Knife Edge and now are culminating it with Crossing the Rubicon. Despite the grimness of it all, especially on the Tyrant of Reason section, I wanted to end on at least a hint of hope and promise with Revelation, and not just resign it all to perdition.

Carl. Prior to the writing and recording sessions of Rubicon, we all felt that we needed to put that final stamp, thematically, on the ELP catalog. And when we looked back, all the way back, we all recognized the general themes and we felt we should end it that way. Certainly, by looking back at the various concepts we've had since Brain Salad Surgery, there are different topics and subjects, historical mostly, that we've used. But for an absolutely final assertion, if you want to call it that, Greg certainly got it right.

Keith. There was something quite audacious about our debut that, I think, frustrated our naysayers to no end. How we were able to construct a band album that was so strongly centered on seemingly non-commercial solo pieces, but then have it resonate so well with the public? One particularly bitter commentator mentioned that if we had zero name recognition or a non-descript band name rather than our names in the band, it wouldn't have worked. It was easy to dismiss it, but maybe he had a point that all three of us were strong enough to take center stage within the band; a case of sour grapes I suppose. I think they were so hopeful and convinced that we would fall short, and then their accusations would be validated. But then it didn't happen, and you know, you can't saw sawdust, so it frustrated them even more. Then of course, being a stadium band, audience participation was seen more as idol worship. It was forgotten, obviously, that all of us had to start out in small, dingy clubs and spent many years there, as well. To many critics, the visuals and spectacles of the big gigs is all they refer to and remember, sadly.

Greg. The most tiresome complaints about ELP were regarding our supposed unceasingly pompous, bombastic, and overblown approaches to our original works, adaptations, and production. Trying to apply moderation with what we were trying to do would not have worked, not at all. We would have been perceived as a bunch of magpies had we not followed through. We did what we felt we needed to do for our style, whatever you want to call it. The punk dogma of less is more reduces the rock aesthetic to two chords and a cloud of dust; we were never going to do that and devolve this band. I always thought that the punk mentality of being deliriously anti-pretentious ironically created its own type of pretentiousness. The mastery of skills invites envy, quite severely, even in musical or artistic circles.

Carl.   I don't think ELP was ever going to lead the parade for our audience to demand some kind of alternative to politics, economics, or whatever the anti-establishment types were calling for, whether it was when we first started out or when punk came to the forefront. ELP, and other UK bands, other progressive bands I suppose, have a certain British-ness that gives the kids some kind of musical identity; I don't really see how it goes any further than that. We weren't preaching alternatives, awareness maybe; we merely focused on the art and the history, which wasn't enough for some.

Keith.   While I'm very aware that it's no longer 1970, I felt obligated to go heavy with the Hammond organ for a final statement. Despite the successful integration of various synths as part of the ELP sound, it is not only my hallmark sound, but the sound of ELP from the very beginning. It is the one electronic instrument that has been with me from day one. I didn't want to be too melodramatic and highlight all the signature sounds I've used in my career. Of course, I will have the usual collection of vintage and modern keyboards at my disposal, especially the Moog; but there is something special about the Hammond and its place in ELP. I love it and, from what I've heard repeatedly over the years, the fans love it as well.

Greg.   I was asked the other day if I had considered the human cloning aspect as far back as when we composed Karn Evil 9. I understand how one could see that, but I think with Karn Evil 9 it was perhaps more related to something like the concept of artificial intelligence where the computer starts recognizing that it could be and do so much better than its creator, and then takes over. It might make an interesting movie someday.   With Rubicon it's more of a tyrannical approach, a sort of hyper-authoritarianism. I was thinking more along the lines of Brave New World [editor – dystopian novel by Aldous Huxley], but looking at it from a slightly different perspective.

Carl. You know, looking back, I'm somewhat convinced that if, early on, we would have simply agreed with the critics that we were merely cannibalizing and vandalizing the classics, making a mockery of it all, they would have been on board with us, right? By doing what we were doing, that we were engaged with others in this notion or movement of tearing down cultural institutions and such? Instead, in interviews we said that we hoped to be a portal, one of several I suppose, for the kids to explore the great European catalog of true quality music, you can call it classical if you want. As soon as we stood by those positions, that was all it took for us to be called soulless, sellouts, pompous, whatever, and that our fans were equally as dumb for accepting it all.

Keith. As we can now take our time with the new album, I look back at the inception of the band's formation and am astounded at the timeline for the first year or so and how we pulled it off back then. I mean, between the debut in November 1970 and Pictures [editor – ELP live album Pictures at an Exhibition] recorded in March 1971, we also found the time to record Tarkus, in addition to playing live concerts. It was slightly mad.

Greg. When you're one of the cogs in the machine, you just keep going, you know? Major events, like big concerts or recording a new album are just seen as business as usual; it's only later you reflect back and wonder how you become immune to what should be huge highlights both personally and professionally. You became a bit desensitized to astounding events, one after the other. But, you just get down to business and put your head down, keep juggling all your responsibilities as best you can, and forge ahead.

Carl. Looking back, that first year or so of ELP was beyond astounding. There was the live performance debut at Plymouth, then the Isle of Wight, recording the debut album, recording Tarkus and Pictures at Newcastle. I'm not saying we were the hardest working band in the music business, but we put in some major, major effort during those first 14 or 15 months. Critics accused us of just waltzing in on our laurels, the whole supergroup nonsense. It was as if we had special powers and everything happened automatically. I'm not saying that having prior recognition didn't help at all; it was a huge benefit in just prompting the public check us out as a new band. But to think for everything that followed, that we just had everything drop in our laps, and that the sales and sold out concerts just simply followed us like a perpetual lucky penny, that is utter nonsense.

Keith. When we started, we discussed amongst ourselves the very real possibility that we would be the object of much, and probably unrelenting, critical scorn. How committed were we to this vision we had? We knew starting out, pre-ELP, that progressive or classical and jazz influenced rock was a sub-culture. Could it expand? I knew from my experience with The Nice that once the word was out of what we were trying to do, that we could key in on overlapping interests, or perhaps a shared history of unique musical interests and tastes. These tastes could easily be seen as exclusionary, or elitist, as it was accused of being. The key was to promote ourselves to an in-group that would have similar, dedicated inclinations as other in-groups, and then it could, maybe, just maybe, take off.

Greg. ELP started on a general principle knowing what we wanted to do, doing it, and not worrying about approval. We actually purposefully wanted to be out of place and out of time; I imagine it was a bit of the hubris and confidence of youth. I'm not saying it all just fell into place automatically, we were completely obsessed; combined with a few key people in our circle, circumstances, and public reaction, it worked.

Carl. A big part of our European heritage, of course, focuses on the tradition of old, you could call it classical, melodies or tunes or themes that were passed on through very primitive means. All music now can be passed on, but we really wanted to make sure that whatever music we could grab ahold of, would not only be passed on, but held aloft and celebrated, not derided. We never thought we were going to change the world, we were looking for others to see what we were doing, and they too could be part of this tradition.

Keith. The Rubicon shows carried with them a very real sense of the approaching end, but not in a negative or sad way. It's the same feeling as when a famous footballer is about to retire, you know, and he steps onto the pitch for his next to the last game. Everybody knows it's not completely over, but it can no longer be ignored. I personally thought the response to the new material was really, really good.

Greg. It had been some time since ELP had covered a subject as dark and perceptible as Crossing the Rubicon. We've had mostly song oriented material compared to the early years, lighter topics, but Rubicon seemed to take us back to Tarkus and Karn Evil, that sense of foreboding. The big difference being that the subject matter is very relevant to today; it's not so much fantasy as it is possibility, near to reality. And also, we had nothing like Are You Ready Eddy? to lighten the mood this time. Was there also an effect knowing that this was our last album and next-to-last tour? Very possibly; we consistently had concerts where the reactions were very enthusiastic, very positive to the new material and the show in general.

Carl. I personally thought the Rubicon shows were fantastic. We are known for extended pieces, concepts, and as a final statement ELP absolutely delivered. It was grand, dark, and ominous, very much how we planned it, and Greg delivered a menacing tale but with a hope for humanity. As one prepares for the final curtain, all the elements of not just the work at hand, but the preparation, this all takes on a new light. All the years prior, you did the exact same thing, but now it's done with a different mindset. While we certainly will do this again individually at some time or another, the circumstances will be different; it certainly won't feel the same to me.

Keith. After Pictures [at an Exhibition] caught a tailwind, the criticisms started becoming more brutal, and pointless. We started getting specifically savaged that we were snobby and playing classical music, or classically inspired music, which supposedly was non-theatrical, meant to be merely listened to. We still got attacked even as we incorporated visuals to function like modern or pop music, entertainment. We took the philosophy that we could both, we could get the audience to listen while also be visually entertaining. But, let it be known, that it was our decision to do so, our choice.

Greg. There's a reason why classical music is often dismissed or disdained as elitist or cold, as was ELP: there is a concern with musicianship, it remains an inherently intricate skill. Many other disciplines in society focus on heightening abilities, proficiency, and advancing the field, which is of course applauded; as it should. But for some reason, music critics couldn't accept the fact that not only were there some musicians in the popular music field that gravitated towards this, but that there was an audience that appreciated the prowess, the virtuosity. Ours was likely the only genre where the artists and fans were mocked and treated like fools.

Carl. The criticisms only bothered me inasmuch that it possibly dissuaded a significant number of people from at least giving us a listen. Personally, I couldn't have cared less; but I know they also ridiculed the fans, which I found offensive. I knew the skills I had and what the others were bringing to the table. There was no reason for me to be aggravated if critics who didn't know a C chord from an electrical cord derided us personally or musically, they had no legitimacy or standing as far as I was concerned.

Keith. When I started down this road of combining classical with rock and then adding jazz influences, I consciously took the classical approach where individuality mattered. I really tried doing something that hadn't been done before on that kind of scale. This was opposed to popular music where an artist was expected to conform to the tastes of the day, the audience. When we started and your audience identified with you that you were purposely differing stylistically from other artists; that was your identity. It's ironic somewhat that we were criticized for being unique, not conforming, by other non-conformists.

Greg. I look at the time when we started, when I started, that rock was on the cusp of a great explosion. You had technology moving forward both in recording and live sound reproduction, and you had the engagement of the record companies, competition for artists, promotion. It was all there, and we were fortunate to be part of that. What I see for the future of popular music is that it seems to be getting less original and that there's a danger there won't be any investment for growth or innovation, a willingness to take a chance. If you look at the fantastic catalog of music from the 1950's to the 1980's that is dearly loved, I'm speaking of popular music of course, what's the motivation to gamble on emerging artists or something potentially trailblazing? There's a real worry that there will never be replication of that great time I've referenced and succeeding generations will only refer to the great music of the past, not of the present, not of their own, their own time.

Carl. The timing of ELP has been unbelievable in many respects, the technology, having companies believe in you that were art-minded, not necessarily purely business-minded. I really don't know if we'll see that again, and I don't mean just for artists in our camp. The possibility for something else unique to not only organically spring up, but then to have the business willing to promote it, sustain it, and give it a chance on a wider scale; I truly have my doubts.

Chapter Eighteen

Extending the Rubicon, 1999

The Finale is Announced

Emerson, Lake, and Palmer

The Alternate History

1975-2000

Prior to the conclusion of the Crossing the Rubicon tour in April 1999, the band announce that the tour has been extended with an emphasis on additional shows outside of North America and Western Europe. Following a short break, this will put the band on the road from June through September. In December, ELP announce they will commence with their final tour which will run from May 2000 through August. The tour, named Emerson, Lake, and Palmer – In the Shadows of the Stars, will consist of eight distinct, rotating set lists focusing on ELP's epic suites, from Pictures at an Exhibition to Crossing the Rubicon. ELP announce that they are committing to play no less than four shows in each of the countries they have visited at least once throughout their career. The US and Western Europe, by fan base default, receive a greater number of shows. The tour will end in the UK, with the final two shows scheduled at the Royal Albert Hall. As happened in 1995 with the ELP 25th Anniversary shows, two shows are eventually added due to popular demand.

Keith. No sooner had we announced our final plans, then the questions started,

"Well Keith, what are you going to do then?" Well, I'll do what I've always done, what's expected of me, and what I expect of myself, write and play music. As a matter of fact, I already have a substantial amount of music completed, much of it for solo piano that I've accumulated over the years. It will be an important part of showing Keith Emerson the composer outside of the structure of ELP.

Greg. When ELP do say their final good night, of course I won't just stop and quit music all together, I don't think that's possible for any musician, be they professional, amateur, or someone who plays for pleasure. It is part of who you are; it moves you. Now, of course, the first thing I will do is what any person does once they've stepped away from the highlight in your life or career; you reflect and take it all in. You have to unwind or uncoil, I suppose. In our case, I know the very first thing we can do the day after is to look back with great satisfaction and remember how indebted we are to so many for our incredibly good fortune over the decades.

Carl. Believe it or not, I'm already getting questions as to what I'm going to do after ELP takes its final bow. And you know, I don't take offense to that question at all. I like being busy and being known for staying busy, I think it's a compliment actually. Some people have hinted that it would be difficult to get out from being known as the drummer for ELP, and I have no problem with that. I do think that I would like to carry on the legacy of ELP's music, but not necessarily only ELP's music, in some format. With my experience as not only a drummer, but what I've gained as an arranger, I would like to give that a try.

Keith. I don't think that revisiting older material is necessarily a bad thing; after all, one matures as a composer and recognizes all sorts of lost opportunities to have developed and expanded upon the original ideas. I often have thought this, probably with Ars Longa [editor – Ars Longa Vita Brevis from The Nice album of the same title] and Tarkus most often. Of course, the question you then always have is, would I have thought of this without the pieces I subsequently composed, or the influences from a live improvisation, or other music I've since absorbed. Where can you, or do you draw the line? It can be a bit dodgy as well as a

213

sensitive matter.

Greg. Many bands, many artists, have thought about rerecording their hits and some have actually done so. It might be for personal reasons, you know, their ideas were outvoted in the studio, or perhaps there were technological limitations at the time which didn't allow them to fulfill what they envisioned. As an artist and fan, you hold dear to the memories of the songs as you first recorded or heard them, as you were going through life, experiencing events. I mean, some of the early Beatles' material might not have been recorded flawlessly, but there's no denying the performance or the magic at the time.

Carl. I think if you bring something new to the table, then why not reinterpret the material? I think the artist can go forward with a clear conscience if they're promoting it as respectful to the original but also adding something truly different. Then the fans know that they're really going to hear something newly interpreted, maybe a bit divergent, rather than just getting a reproduction. The question is though, how different will it be, and can and will it resonate; only time will tell.

Keith. I've often been asked if I feel that ELP got short-changed when it came to single success, chart success. Obviously ELP benefitted from the early days of FM radio in America, you know, pieces like Pictures [editor – ELP live album Pictures at an Exhibition] getting played in their entirety on the radio; but those days eventually went away; quite quickly it seems, sadly. But, all things considered, for the kind of band that ELP is, very often thanks to Greg's songs, I believe we had very good exposure. I'm sure we gained more than a few fans who maybe bought the singles like Lucky Man, From the Beginning, or I Believe in Father Christmas, and then heard the B-sides or the other tracks and became intrigued.

Greg. I think ELP has been treated fairly when it comes to singles, by both the record company and the public. I mean, it's not as if our albums were always sprinkled with radio ready material, you know? Early on it was mostly my songs, and we even had a bit of unexpected chart success in the US with Nutrocker [editor – US #70], but then we branched out with Fanfare [editor – Fanfare for the

214

Common Man, UK #2] and then with Touch and Go the single [editor – US #60] we had chart exposure and mixed media success in America. I do think that there were some songs in the ELP catalog that were worthy, high-quality songs that perhaps deserved singles' recognition. Songs like Still You Turn Me On, I Don't Know Why, and even Lay Down Your Guns or Affairs of the Heart, as well as Keith's song On My Way Home; they all had some mainstream potential, but it just didn't play out that way.

Carl. As Greg came into his own as the balladeer relatively early on, I figured that was our best chance at a so-called hit single, whatever that really means. I mean, we were fortunate to have gotten massive airplay during those wonderful days of album oriented rock, and that wasn't necessarily only the charting singles. We calculated that a relatively guaranteed way to leave our mark globally early on, to establish a long-term career, was through touring, right? One can't bank on a massive, hit single, especially in our case where we really only had one opportunity at a single per album, which was quite obvious. It could happen, and sometimes it did, but we chose to have control of our own destiny by leaving a worldwide imprint as great as possible with touring, which wasn't always easy. Obviously we didn't tour everywhere at first, but we hit the markets that we thought would help us in that regard, of course I'm referring to America.

Keith. It was a pleasure playing Crossing the Rubicon, not only from the reaction that it received, but that we kind of went back to the origins of ELP with this kind of dark and cautionary tale Greg came up with. Following Brain Salad Surgery we focused on relatively more positive themes, Pirates, Memoirs, The Miracle, let me see, and For Those Who Dare of course. I'm hoping that the quality of the piece gained it some attention, but I understand that mysterious and ominous pieces are what ELP is known for and perhaps that's what fans like to see, or liked to see again.

Greg. I do feel that we reached back in ELP's history of thematic pieces with Rubicon; if nothing else fans sensed it touched on our earlier pieces like Tarkus and that they saw this not only as ELP's final album, but that the story we've told

215

throughout our albums now has concluded, albeit it somewhat with an unresolved, or open ending. And while this was not done consciously, I can see how pieces like Knife Edge and Karn Evil lay the groundwork for this concept of humanity that has become heartless and there is no redemption. Man continues to treat his kind and his environment with great contempt, so what's the solution? That's what Rubicon addresses; although I do hope that the final segment of Revelation reveals a hope that while in the face of seemingly infinite, corrupted power, humanity at its purest can prevail.

Carl. If ELP would have continued on, I do believe that Rubicon would have cemented itself within the ELP catalog up there with Tarkus and Karn Evil; it was sufficiently musically powerful and thematically gripping to do so. Obviously it was never going to have that broad appeal chart-wise considering we're 28 or 29 years on, but within our segment we were very, very happy with it as a final ELP statement. There just is something very special about ELP and its presentation of dramatic pieces, it suits all three of our strengths very well.

Keith. It is rather astounding how quickly public tastes in music shift, and have shifted. You know, classical music dominated up to the 1800's or so, which is interesting because it actually and continually was the music of the time. Not necessarily all the popular music, you know, the kind you heard in pubs and such. There was much music by commission, and that really is the same approach now, except it's a record company. I think that so much popular music, with the exception of jazz, the harmonic exploration is so lacking, sadly. Even with similar music forms, the use of instruments and voice is so drastically different, limited.

Keith. I see an interesting relationship between jazz and bebop and then rock and so-called progressive rock. Technique and speed were seen as contradictions when it came to the ability to relate, by fans of traditional jazz, I suppose. Modern jazz, bebop, was quite violent really, and detached. And this has been the accusation of progressive rock as well. I think both have this ability to relate to the expression of certain feelings, not just personal emotions, just like how rock in the beginning was consciously tapping into youth discontent and casting off old customs and such. I mean, simpler music probably communicates or resonates more quickly and more broadly, but maybe the emphasis on technique and complexity resulted in a gap between artist and audience. Then in our case, when you see the further separation caused by performing in large venues, it stopped being communal and thus apparently, elitist. But I think that's not necessarily so, if anything the community that could relate to that music, was broadened by virtue of the audiences we did attract. From that viewpoint I think ELP, perhaps unintentionally, has such a variety of material that prevents us from completely falling in that trap. I suppose that many of Greg's pieces gave us that popular engagement that allowed us to do pieces like Tarkus, and reach more than we perhaps would have. What this will be like in another 20 or 30 years? Will pieces like Tarkus still be seen as radical and appreciated, or merely a reflection of the moment? I mean, I suppose there is a limit to what the public is willing to entertain, since art is of the time.

Greg. Being part of the 'rock is rebellion' generation, it is amusing to look at one's own journey and suddenly recognize that how you yourself hated so-called old things, but now cherish what was new and original to you. As time moves on, there's always a new group of young haters.

Carl. I think Keith was continuously building, creating his vision, and he attained a plateau as a composer with The Nice, he's said so himself. And then it was a journey for him to find the keys or elements to complete this vision. He understood that he was working to make the fusing of styles resonate and that it could potentially appeal on a large scale rather than just with a bunch of bohemians. All three of us, seeing what was being created, now understood the potency of using European-based music, music that was engrained in the culture, in a new setting, that being rock. What helped tremendously is that with just the three of us, we had to band together, we couldn't afford to have a fall guy, like a Brian Jones [editor — Rolling Stones guitarist]. And besides, we were fortunate that unlike other bands where they have to turn a member's obsessions and chaos into something workable, let alone dealing with the personal problems, our discipline and instincts allowed us to be positively creative, and move forward at a very rapid pace as our early years showed.

Keith. So many observers got it wrong that they thought that our adaptations of classical pieces was a refutation of what the original composer had done, and that we allegedly knew better…this was so preposterous. Our arrangements of classical pieces were a demonstration that these great pieces could be interpreted in a number of ways. It wasn't only rock critics that we dealt with, but also classical music enthusiasts who saw our works as a sort of pillage and plunder, you know? I mean, I can understand holding these pieces dear, I do. If we were only doing this as part of some vast, unsympathetic commercial enterprise, I would understand, but it obviously wasn't that. Art and culture are intertwined, and we treated it very seriously. Roll Over Beethoven [editor – Chuck Berry song] was seen as some great statement, imagine the outcry if we had done something mocking these overtly simple and unimaginative musical structures.

Greg. Would our brand of rock have found a footing at any other time that it did? Early rock benefitted from the explosion in mass media, probably in the 1950's, especially with television coming to the forefront and supplying a visual representation. And then of course, you had the LP and a record player and all of a sudden there was a consumer market rather than records just headed to the jukebox. The rocket really launched with the mass introduction of 45's which were affordable for young people. We arrived in the wake of that when all those early business models were finally getting some footing and the companies could be adventurous and had money to spend, luckily for us. So yes, we certainly benefitted as well as having people in key positions that were art-minded, not just looking at balance sheets. As time went on I think you saw a repeat of those wild early years, but it was repeating either through different mediums, such as video, or the internet, but then artistic basis from the companies went missing.

Carl. When you look at art rock, progressive rock, symphonic rock, whatever you'd like to call it, I always found it fascinating that it had such a Euro-centric origin, you know? I mean, sure, you had classical music, which is of European heritage; we've all heard that explanation of the UK being between the US and continental

Europe. But I thought for sure it would have had the chance to develop, not necessarily originally, but more quickly in the US. They were the only major country not devastated by World War 2, so one would think that it, and other elements in society with a futuristic outlook, would have flourished there without all the constraints and shortages we had that lasted long, long after the war ended. But, what's interesting is that after the war, there was a renewed emphasis on leisure, a respite from the horrific consequences of war. I think that with progressive rock, there was the fan element – as a result of that experience, I believe – that took life and leisure seriously, and that would be in music as well. And much the same as with early rock and teenagers claiming it as their music, we had fans that took our music, and other bands like us, very seriously, very personally. It translated to meaning and experience, especially with the classical leanings that we were derided for. It wasn't highbrow or lowbrow, it was everyday.

Keith. I think there's a certain hierarchy in music, popular music, just as there as in any field or art. And like, say, with paintings or sculptures, I suppose that which is a bit more abstract or conceptual requires more attention and attracts a different audience that is merely looking at instant access, or an expression. I'm proud to say we've had both, with our concept pieces and then with Greg's tunes. We never went full bore either direction, mostly, it was a balance that occurred naturally.

Chapter Nineteen

In England's Green and Pleasant Land, 2000

The Finale

Emerson, Lake, and Palmer

The Alternate History

1975-2000

As planned, ELP's farewell tour starts in April of 2000 and lasts through August. True to their promise, the eight setlists are rotated through as the tour progresses, with the commitment to multiple shows played in the countries ELP has visited over the course of their touring career. As the tour progresses, some countries' show numbers are cut back; this happens in France, Spain, and Sweden, while there are shows added in Italy, Hungary, and Bulgaria.

Keeping in line with tradition, ELP also interpolate various incognito acoustic shows, but only in the US, and are much abbreviated from such past, more numerous shows. Breaking with the tradition of their past incognito acoustic tours, they play material not only from the ELP catalog also but from their previous bands as well. The band advertises themselves randomly as PP Armpit and The Mice, In the Hall of the Manticore, Wash and Blow, or Greg's Nutters.

As the tour finishes traversing the globe, the ELP traveling show reaches their homeland for the last time in early August 2000. While preparing for their career finale at the Royal Albert Hall starting on August 29 (the 30th anniversary of the Isle of Wight Festival), they make an unexpected announcement. ELP will play a one-off show at the Plymouth Guildhall on August 23, the 30th anniversary of their debut at that very same venue, where they will replicate that historic, first show. Holders of copies of the original tickets to that show, or the Isle of Wight show that followed, will get in for free by pre-registering and having their ticket's authenticity validated.

ELP's final string of four shows commence on August 29 at the Royal Albert Hall. The setlist is as follows –

Tarkus

Pictures at an Exhibition

Karn Evil 9

Pirates

The Miracle

Crossing the Rubicon

Encore - Fanfare for the Common Man

The setlist remains consistent over all four shows with one, final exception. For the very last show, following the ending of Fanfare for the Common Man, the band remains at their instruments. When the applause eventually subsides, they launch into Jerusalem, played faithfully just as it was recorded on Brain Salad Surgery.

Keith. There was no realistic way we could come up with the perfect setlist, you know? How do you create a two-hour set from something as vast as our back catalog? Some material undoubtedly is going to be left out, someone will be disappointed. We experimented with each of us having a solo spot after an opening number or two, then maybe two or three of our most popular extended pieces, sort of giving you a snapshot of what makes ELP tick. The three elements individually and then combined, the complete workings of Emerson, Lake, and Palmer. But, let's be honest. Where do you begin? Greg has so much material, how does he choose? We have a number of lengthy suites, where do you start? So then we finally decided on creating multiple setlists, and with the way this tour is arranged, if you're a fan in Italy and you like Tarkus, there's a chance you'll get to hear it. We do realize there's always a chance someone is not going to hear their favorite piece, and for a final goodbye, I do feel a sense of contrition. I hope we can make up for it by simply putting on the best and memorable shows that we can.

Greg. Management suggested replicating our Brain Salad Surgery tour setlist, which of course became the Welcome Back record [editor – triple live album Welcome Back My Friends to the Show That Never Ends]. But while that was a, if not the, great high point in ELP's career, there's too much material post-1974 to ignore. So we then spent a lot of time not only deciding, but playing and relearning so much of our legacy material. We were also very honest with each other. We know what has resonated with our fans, and what hasn't, even if it's something we personally were somewhat fond of.

Carl. We certainly didn't take the easy way out in preparing the farewell tour. We could have simply come up with a single setlist and taken a swing at what we felt should be played and be done with it, which is what most bands probably do. But, you know, ELP has never taken the easy way out. So we created this multi-headed monster of setlists. What I found so interesting is that at first we were lamenting a bit all the work we had to do. But as we started rehearsals, the music came together quite quickly, and we actually enjoyed not only playing all the old material, but we also found ourselves not worn down by playing the same bits over and over. We unintentionally created a musical environment that we didn't tire of.

Keith. I must admit, it was beyond daunting knowing we had multiple setlists for this tour, and while the rehearsals all went smoothly, we had some very earnest last minute discussions if we should do this. But, ELP has always gone for the grand execution, going that extra step that other bands might dare not consider. As the shows clicked off, it felt like we were giving the fans their attention and money's worth.

Greg. The catalog is so engrained in all of us, once the muscle memory returned; we all just went on a sort of auto-pilot. It certainly was more than a bit of work, I assure you, but the results were gratifying. The sheer volume of historical work we've presented has been, even for those of us in the midst of it, breathtaking.

Carl. I'm not exaggerating when I say that the music has literally become part of my DNA. 30 years on, I still know every break, every accent, and every time signature change. The key in group rehearsal, of course, is fine tuning that unspoken communication we have. Sometimes we feel the need to extend a break, we've done that on Eruption [editor – from Tarkus] and Hellburners [editor – from Conquering Tide], for example. Once the piece starts, it's automatic for me, and I've always been that way. It's the result of a total immersion into the material once we had committed to writing and recording it.

Keith. When we decided on the final setlist, there was some thinking of incorporating another element, or elements you know, to make one of the concept pieces we selected unique or more complete in relation to our catalog. Sort of like what Greg did with Epitaph [editor – King Crimson song] on Battlefield [editor – from ELP's Tarkus album]. We thought about adding an element from Conquering Tide [editor – ELP albums] to Pirates [editor – ELP's album of the same name]. But, we decided that we needed to play the albums as they were created and recorded. Creating a pastiche, I don't know, it certainly can be effective, but not for a grand finale.

Greg. The purity of the finale was a necessity, I believe. The pieces we selected are so integral to the history of ELP; we didn't want to dilute the integrity of the pieces. Of course it was tempting to toss in that, that, and the other. Keith had

223

some ideas, and we considered expanding upon The Miracle [editor – from ELP's Touch and Go album] as well, I had a couple of extra verses that didn't make the final cut. But the discussions always came back 'round to performing the pieces, for the last time as ELP, as they're known with the excitement that comes with live performance.

Carl. I was quite happy with the setlist we ultimately decided on. Yes, it is heavy on the early years, but there's no denying that was the time when ELP made its mark. We were on an incredible roll those first four or five years. But, having said that, we are proud of all the material, and it was nice to see The Miracle represent our middle period and then of course Crossing the Rubicon [editor – ELP's final album] representing the closure of ELP's concept canon.

Keith. It was very tempting to come up with an excess of production for this tour that would demonstrate everything ELP was known, loved, and despised for at the same time. You know, an orchestra, even a small one, ballet dancers, rotating pianos or revolving drum sets, a flight of Spitfires, cannons, lasers, spaceships [laughs], whatever, as long as it was over the top. But we always found ourselves going back to the beginning, looking back at what we did that got us noticed. We simply played, and when we did, we didn't need anything as it was uniquely ELP, and it still is.

Greg. We've come full circle in a way, both as how we presented ourselves as a band and individually. We started out with mostly minimal production, as most bands do. Then of course as we gained in popularity and the budgets grew and all the special effects that followed, the lighting proscenium, quad with the Brain Salad Surgery tour, the occasional orchestra, quad again with the Touch and Go tour, dramatic backdrops with Conquering Tide, and probably a few things I've forgotten. And now, we're back to where we were, showing that as a band, effects or not, it's the music that propels it all.

Carl. Preparing for the farewell tour, there was something in each of us where we said, it was our playing that got us where we were then, and it's gotten us where we are now. We're approaching it with the same tenacity we did then, albeit with
224

substantially more wisdom. We will always play for effect and impression.

Keith. Progressive rock has left its mark, ELP left its mark. I mean, what else could we ask for, really. Even before ELP, the three of us were fortunate to have been there at the right time as the movement seemed to blossom. For those of us in the middle of it all, we were surrounded by the right personalities, and it propelled us along to ELP.

Greg. What is the legacy of progressive rock or of ELP? Not just bringing classical music to the masses for listening enjoyment, but also music that could have been forgotten or was limited in exposure. But it was also to reinforce the idea that this is music to be played and expanded upon, without hesitation. ELP has always been aware of this and has done both throughout our career.

Carl. I think our music has had its heyday, but that's not only the case with prog as a genre. Many other unique musical styles have had their spike in popularity and then disappear from the mainstream into the background. Some will always be there while others are mostly forgotten. The difference, I believe, is that music with substance will endure. For example, jazz will never be as popular in the US as it was in the 1940's, but it still exists and has a following. Strangely enough, prog has now also returned to how it was conceived, which was art-driven. When it did enter the mainstream, it eventually seemed to get watered-down and maybe was abandoned by its core fans and even the artists themselves. Going with the times, I suppose. But, when the popularity waned, it then became art-focused again and more specialist. Its story is not one alone in the artistic world.

Keith. The big crossroads in the band's history? If this would be something after the band got rolling and getting the three of us together, I would probably say it was the writing and recording of Tarkus. I think for those that know about the band's history, it's a bit obvious. At first, Greg and I certainly weren't on the same page, but it was amazing how it eventually all came together. I truly never tire of playing it, and it really became the piece it is from all three of us being completely on board.

Greg. My view of the major turning point or points in ELP's history? Well, there are several of course, the obvious ones everyone knows about. I personally think that what ultimately allowed us to successfully sustain our career was the decision to create Brain Salad Surgery in a live environment. We reinstituted that intimacy in working closely together, going over every detail bit by bit. While we have recorded many fine pieces since then, we needed to internally reestablish ourselves as a live band that can play the studio material just as accurately and dynamically as it was recorded. While Trilogy is an ELP high point for me artistically, we couldn't completely deliver that record live as we had done with our previously recorded material, which was very unfortunate. The Brain Salad Surgery record was the successful harnessing of energy and experience that truly became career establishing for ELP, in my opinion. We shouldn't forget that the Touch and Go record was also key in ELP's career, a sort of a comeback as it's been referred to; I prefer to call it a reestablishing.

Carl. ELP has been at a career boiling point several times, but nothing that I think would have meant the true ending of the band, with the possible exception of the recording of Tarkus. It's not news, but we had a well-received debut, both live and on record, but we weren't really established, which made Tarkus hanging in the balance a very real concern. A secondary point, I would probably say was the recording and releasing of I Believe in Father Christmas as ELP, the Winter's Light album. It was a bit of a worry what kind of interruption it would have been had we taken a true, extended break after Welcome Back [editor – live album Welcome Back My Friends to the Show That Never Ends].

Keith. We always enjoyed the incognito tours so much, and it's been a decade tradition for ELP, so we wanted to do it one more time. Carl was the one who suggested that we could broaden out a bit and should also do material from our pre-ELP bands, any one of them, which I thought was a wonderful idea. There is a bit of a reference this time to our 25th anniversary shows, but that was a natural development. The big dilemma is, as always, choosing the tracks from a pool that is absolutely enormous.

Greg. When ELP formed, we were very, very deliberate and persistent that we were staking out our own identity, both live and on record, and that we would rarely, if ever, resort to any pre-ELP tunes. Rondo was the exception, of course; if nothing else we wanted to prove we could do it better. But we are now in a different era for the band; it's a time of reflection rather than getting ready to climb mountains.

Carl. Much like the 25th ELP anniversary concerts, I decided that if we are ever going to do something similar but with the acoustic concept, we had to do it now of course. It's a way of acknowledging our combined legacies, to showcase the musical lineages, and to be respectful of the past while embracing the current. We're celebrating the end of our road by looking back at the end of the other roads that carried us here.

Keith. I was recently interviewed by a mainstream journalist, who probably wasn't even born when ELP was formed, which isn't a problem really. As he was fumbling through his papers and backpack, he asked me how I felt about ELO coming to the end of the road. I told him Jeff and I are looking forward to some memorable concerts, and putting on a great show for the fans. He continued looking at his notes and his mobile and asked if we were just going to play all the hits or if we had any surprises planned. I told him, absolutely, we'll be playing nothing but the radio hits, but then I told him that I would share a surprise that we have planned. He became quite excited and prepared to take some notes. I let him in on the secret that we were planning on playing Geno Astaire's famous piano concerto, and while we hadn't played it live in quite some time, we will be playing all three impressions. He excitedly scribbled some notes, thanked me for my time, and ran off. So, yeah, millions of records and hundreds of concerts later, here we are...still.

Greg. Let's see, what have I heard over the years what some our songs were titled. There's Closer to the Leaving, Jeremy Blender, and few others I can't remember right now; but there is my personal favorite, The Barber, Ian.

Carl. Well, what can you do regarding the most generic press coverage where you can tell no one has the slightest idea about the band. The most one could hope for is that you get the opportunity to set people straight, measure by measure, and pray that they get most of it right for general consumption.

Keith. It was Carl's idea to play the Plymouth Guildhall to commemorate the anniversary and I do admit it was a wonderful idea, and quite emotional. It was also an exercise in restraint to remain true to that show knowing what we know now.

Greg. On stage at the Guildhall, looking out at the audience, you really can't fathom 30 years went by. Your mind goes back to not only what you were doing, but what your thoughts were for yourself and the band. You reflect on the people who were in your life, the ones who stayed by your side, some who are no longer with you. And while the hall had certainly changed, I had this very satisfying feeling that ELP now also was part of its great history.

Carl. The Plymouth Guildhall commemorative show was a very well-intentioned idea that turned into a bit of a farce. We had the very honest purpose of recognizing or honoring those who came to that first show, and doing something special for them. At first, the thought was who really hangs on to a concert ticket for 30 years? But, our management did some research, and some people really do. But, how many would have for this particular show which certainly was a bit in the background at the time, you know? So, we then expanded it to those who would have a ticket from the Isle of Wight Festival. We thought we would improvise our way through, as to who gets to go and who doesn't, but it turned into a shambles. All of a sudden we were presented with so many tickets that wouldn't have even been available or sold for the Plymouth show, and then the number of Isle of Wight tickets was a mudslide, too much to process. I imagine it's a bit of flattery, but still, we finally had to make some on-the-spot decisions and did the best we could. The very least we could do was to make sure that the tickets we did disperse were provided to individuals, not any agencies.

Keith. To choose a setlist for the final shows at the Royal Albert Hall was, to be honest, more than a bit heart-wrenching. Obviously we're not going to do eight final shows, but we had to come up with the ultimate, within reason of course,

228

ELP setlist. Once we started examining the catalog, it all worked its way out. Of course, the set list is a bit longer than the typical show we did for the final tour, which is why we considered having an intermission; if there was any time to do so, this would be it.

Greg. It was a task and a half, building the ultimate ELP setlist with all the constraints one has. But, we've encountered similar challenges over the years, as the catalog started building. Once we were solidly past the band's first five or six years, into the Fanfare and Pirates era or so we already had to drop material. And now, 30 years later, there was even more material to consider for inclusion or omission.

Carl. I didn't see selecting the songs to be played as much of a dilemma, it was actually a joy choosing the cream of the crop as it were. Sure, there are pieces that we as individuals are fond of, but we're looking at representing the band in the fans' eyes in the best possible way. It was a pleasure knowing how much the fans will be enjoying it.

Keith. You know, from the first time that Greg and I played together, somewhat accidentally at the Fillmore West, and the time that the three of us played together for the very first time in that tiny rehearsal room in Soho Square, there always was this spark, this kind of mysterious energy. It was there from the beginning, it never left us, from day one up until the last note of Jerusalem; the power of ELP was always present.

Greg. I say this with all the humility possible, but I can't think of an ELP show where we weren't fully committed to putting on the best performance, and just as equally, where we didn't rightfully criticize ourselves and each other when it was deserved. Of course, we've had some nights where the sound may have been uneven, or we had a technical problem, an out of tune guitar, you know. But our determination to be fully engaged for a show never, ever wavered.

Carl. Whatever differences we may have had when we were recording, or something that came up on tour, we always put it aside to focus on the work or show at hand. Whether we were recording Tarkus or Conquering Tide, or if we were about to start a show discussing a matter, we always put it in a box while we took care of business. I can't understand this notion you hear of some bands that have members who purposefully try to sabotage the show or try to make someone look bad simply because they're irate. I mean, you're supposed to be a professional; you should always treat your vocation with respect. And then these same individuals wonder why, despite their talents, they can't seem to get a call. At the end of the day, no one wants to be around someone like that.

Keith. When we had finalized the finale show's setlist, we immediately were considering a possible surprise ending for the very, very last song we'd be playing on stage. It sounds easy, but when you really start pondering the matter, it really isn't. We've been ending with Fanfare [editor – Fanfare for the Common Man] for years, quite happily and appropriately I might add. We briefly considered Farewell to Arms as our very final piece. It's a very heartfelt song, and it seems that as we enter a new millennium that it's a new world, a new order; but history can be quite fickle. But then we thought, what captures the history, the essence, and the meaning and motivation of ELP. It had to be Jerusalem, no question. As far as our greater history, if we succeeded in incorporating various elements, especially European music, within rock, that is subjective. But I can honestly say we gave it our all, without exception.

Greg. We hadn't played Jerusalem regularly for several tours. Obviously it was on a popular album and it always resonates with our British audiences, but it would be eventually dropped on other tours or when we toured places other than the UK. We considered a number of tracks for our surprise finale; Show Me the Way to Go Home was a bit too predictable, and that really was only a track from the acoustic shows. As the absolute final number performed by ELP, we wanted to play something that not only sums up our personal and artistic origins, but something that signifies and represents ELP and how we came to have our philosophies of music, culture, and performance manifested itself in our original material. We had to pick Jerusalem. While we certainly had egos, we realized that even with our original concept pieces that drew on classical elements, we
230

were standing on the shoulders of giants.

Carl. Jerusalem will always be an amazing piece of music, and thoroughly British. Although it of course has a religious bent to it, it's technically not a hymn. I think what attracted us to it was the symbolism, in a variety of ways, which can only be British, you know. Does Jerusalem signify peace and harmony, perhaps some kind of universal, Anglophile humanity? It's possible. But we know what it has meant for ELP. It signifies our musical origins and desire of musical exploration, our willingness to pursue excellence in the face of being hated for our virtues. As such, we hope that our music has added to and revealed the light, power, and history of European music to the world itself.

Epilogue

There's no escape from this band.

Greg Lake, 1992

ABC In Concert

Printed in Great Britain
by Amazon

48758857R00129